Cooking for the Wayward Diabetic

by the same author

★

A COOK'S NOTEBOOK

Cooking for the Wayward Diabetic

❊

LILY MACLEOD

Certificates in Cookery and Dietetics
Glasgow and West of Scotland College
of Domestic Science

with carbohydrate values calculated by
Iris Holland Rogers
formerly Dietetics Adviser to the British Diabetic Association

FABER AND FABER
London · Boston

First published in 1960
by Faber and Faber Limited
3 Queen Square, London W.C.1
Reprinted with corrections 1966
Second edition 1971
First published in Faber Paperbacks 1979
Printed in Great Britain by
Whitstable Litho, Straker Brothers Ltd.
All rights reserved

British Library Cataloguing in Publication Data

MacLeod, Lily
Cooking for the wayward diabetic. – 2nd ed.
  1. Cookery for diabetics
  I. Title
  641.5'63   RC662

ISBN 0–571–11448–2

WISHES

Go, little book, and wish to all
Flowers in the garden, meat in the hall,
A bin of wine, a spice of wit,
A house with lawns enclosing it,
A living river by the door,
A nightingale in the sycamore!

R.L.S.

Contents

---❁---

Author's Preface

We all know such people as the wayward diabetic. Exhorted not to do this or that because of their health, they go gaily on, defying many of the rules—and getting away with it—while their more orthodox friends, who follow instructions to the letter, look a trifle sad.

My husband has been a diabetic for thirty years. From the very first, when his diet was much more restricted than it is now, he never made a burden of his complaint; nor has he ever made his illness an excuse for not doing anything. He has never stuck rigidly to a weighed diet. Even had he been a stickler for accuracy in such matters, it would have been difficult for him to carry it out because, until five years ago, he lived more often in other people's houses than he did in his own. One can't exactly demand priority treatment under these conditions! His puddings (junket, milk jelly or custard in those days) were always cooked with saccharine and for the rest he enjoyed a good mixed diet and plenty of it, for he has always been a hearty eater.

He has kept wonderfully well over the years, due more to his outlook on life than to any special care. His spells in hospital have been few—three in all—and he has never been in a coma. Always a heavy meat eater, he also loves fruit and vegetables, but seldom touches sweets or cake except when he feels shaky. He is neither a teetotaller nor a non-smoker. He tests himself fairly regularly and adjusts his insulin a unit or two either way, when necessary. What does upset his balance more than anything is emotional stress, not to mention too long a spell without food. Diabetes, he tells me, runs in his family.

Unorthodox foods that he demands occasionally are such things as sausages, rice,* macaroni, bananas.* If I don't put them on the menu he gets them himself *and* cooks them. His excuse for these flights from reality is this: that he doesn't always want to be reminded of his complaint; so I threaten to send him back to Bart's, where he was first treated, as a specimen diabetic who thrives, in spite of his waywardness!

For many years he took insulin twice a day. Now he has changed to Insulin Zinc Suspension Lente (80 units per ml.) of which he takes about 21 units each morning, making his daily insulin 84 units in all.

Apart from diabetic chocolate, jam and sweetening we use no diabetic preparations. Because of its high protein, fruit and vegetable content a diabetic's diet is in itself costly. He likes bread made with ordinary or wholemeal flour and eats apples*as a filler when he is very hungry.

Mostly, the sweetening we use is in tablet form, but the liquid sweetening is handy for use with cold sweets or to adjust the flavour at the last. That is why both kinds are mentioned in some recipes. Sweetening, like salt, is largely a matter of individual taste. I am inclined to undersweeten because, to me, food that is over-sweetened is as deadened and devoid of flavour as food that is too salt.

Preface

This little book is not meant to woo any diabetic from his or her way of life, nor is it meant to encourage anyone to defy the doctor. It is but a statement of fact. We have all got to earn our living, so even diets have to be tailored to our own particular way of life.

Our own meal-times are as follows:

BREAKFAST, 8.30. Grapefruit, orange or stewed fruit, porridge or cereal, bacon, eggs, etc., bread and butter.

11 o'clock. A cup of coffee, tea, Marmite or Oxo—he should have biscuit and cheese but he never does.

DINNER, 12.30. A cup of soup always in winter, with the usual meat and sweet to follow.

HIGH TEA, about 5.15 p.m. The usual Scottish high tea with fish, eggs, or something equally savoury as the main dish, bread, rolls and fresh fruit.

LAST THING. Tea, cocoa or clear soup, biscuit and cheese, apples and usually an orange.

Sometimes he has a cup of tea in the afternoon with a piece of buttered bread, sometimes not. Diabetics really need a mid-afternoon snack.

One good tablespoon of cooked rice contains 10 gm. of carbo-hydrate, 1 small banana 10 gm. and 1 medium-sized apple 10 gm.

Packed Meals

Whereas we ordinary mortals can go for long spells without food, not so diabetics on insulin or tablets. Food is their driving power and even a short time past their allotted meal time can mean a reaction. Diabetics going for car or train journeys should always carry food even though they expect to be at journey's end in time for a meal. Accidents can happen and leave one stranded in unlikely places. Right through this little book I have noted where the recipes could be used for carried meals. Here is a list.

Packed Meals

Savoury Food

As a diabetic's meat course is much the same as in ordinary diet, this section is a selection of recipes that we have from time to time as a change. It includes soups, fish, meat and egg dishes embracing dinner, high tea and supper.

CABBAGE SOUP

2–3 lb. pickled belly pork, 1 small firm cabbage which should weigh ¾–1 lb. after trimming, 1 large onion, chunks of mixed vegetables if required, 4 pints cold water, salt and pepper.

Remove very coarse outside leaves from the cabbage, cut in quarters and wash well. Put the pork and cabbage on in cold water to barely cover, bring to boil and throw away the water. This is in case the pork is very salt and the cabbage strong in flavour.

Return the pork to the pan, add the measured cold water, bring to boil and simmer for about one hour. Add the diced onion and the cabbage, also diced, with chunks of mixed vegetables such as carrot, turnip and onion if these are desired for a second vegetable. Add salt if needed and leave to simmer for a further 45–60 minutes, or until the pork and large vegetables are cooked. Remove the pork and serve it separately, garnished with the whole vegetables. Skim the fat from the soup, add freshly ground pepper and serve. Four to six servings.

This is an adaptation of *Garbure*, a peasant soup from the south of France. The original version should have ½ pint soaked haricot beans cooked in it, or 3 or 4 diced potatoes, as well as vegetables such as peas, broad or runner beans while in season. For our purpose we do without the starch and it is still good. *Negligible carbohydrate.*

QUICK AND EASY BORSCH

2 tablespoonsful of finely grated raw beetroot, about 2 tablespoonsful of malt or tarragon vinegar, a morsel of finely chopped onion (optional) and a medium-sized tin of consommé.

Pour the vinegar over the grated beetroot. Place it in the saucepan with the onion and cover with a little of the consommé. Let it simmer very gently for a few minutes then add the rest of the consommé, bring to boil and serve. It can be strained free of the beetroot if desired. A blob of whipped cream, soured with yoghurt or vinegar, should be served with each soup-cup. *This recipe makes 2 servings with negligible grams of carbohydrate.*

TOMATO CELERY SOUP

8 oz. tomatoes (about 5 small), 4 oz. coarse outside pieces of celery, 1 small onion peeled and chopped, 1 clove, a pinch of powdered basil, 1 pint stock, 1 oz. margarine, salt, pepper, very tiny scraps of bayleaf and thyme.

Melt the margarine. Add the onion and add celery washed and diced. Toss in the fat and leave to cook (covered) over a gentle heat for 20 minutes. Stir from time to time. Add the tomatoes, washed and chopped, along with the herbs and a pinch of salt. Cover and leave to cook for a further 10 minutes, stirring occasionally and adding a little stock if it gets sticky, which it shouldn't. Finally add the stock, bring to boil and simmer for 15 minutes, when the celery should be soft enough to sieve. Season to taste, rub through a sieve, return the sieved soup to the rinsed pan and let it get boiling hot. Adjust seasoning and serve. Two servings.

A nice refreshing soup. The first time I made it was to use up odd scraps of celery and some squashy end-of-season tomatoes. *Negligible carbohydrate.*

COLD TOMATO CREAM SOUP

½ pint tomato pulp, ¼ pint milk, a level teaspoon of very finely chopped raw onion and the same of horse-radish cream, salt and pepper, about 2 tablespoons freshly chopped parsley which can be omitted, but it is nice.

Let the pulp get quite cold. Whisk in the milk, onion and horse-radish cream. Season to taste, add the parsley if available, chill thoroughly in the refrigerator and serve icy cold. Two servings. A lovely soup, thick and a nice pink, but it must be well chilled.

To make the tomato pulp, cook ¾ lb. sliced tomato in a covered saucepan over a slow heat until soft enough to sieve. Cook with it a little sliced onion, a level teaspoonful of basil, pinches of powered cloves and seasoning to taste.

Or, cook a breakfastcupful of tinned tomato with the basil until mushy, and sieve. *Each serving contains 5 gm. of carbohydrate.*

LETTUCE AND CELERY SOUP

2 breakfastcupfuls of diced celery, 1 onion peeled and diced, 1 blade mace, 3 breakfastcupfuls of stock or cold water, 1 breakfastcupful of diced lettuce and 1–2 table-spoonsful of freshly chopped parsley if available.

Put the celery, onion and mace in the pan with the measured stock or water. Bring to boil, season to taste and simmer gently until the celery is tender enough to sieve—about an hour. Strain the soup, squashing through as much of the celery as possible. Return the strained soup to the pan, add the lettuce, bring to boil and simmer for about 10 minutes. Add salt if necessary, freshly ground black pepper, stir in the parsley and serve. Two servings.

I use coarse outside stalks of celery for this soup. Don't let the celery boil too fast or the liquid will evaporate. *Negligible carbohydrate.*

Savoury Food

WATERCRESS SOUP

1 bunch watercress, 1 4-in. piece of finely chopped celery (optional) or 2 or 3 coarse lettuce leaves, 1 small onion peeled and chopped, 3 cups white stock or water, salt, pepper and 2 tablespoonfuls of cream.

Wash and chop the watercress, leaf and stalk. Put it in the pan with the onion, lettuce and celery, add the stock or water, bring to boil, season to taste and simmer slowly until the watercress can be sieved—about 45 minutes. Strain the soup and squash the cress through. Return the soup to the rinsed pan, adjust seasoning and heat until boiling. Put a tablespoonful of cream into each cup, pour the boiling soup over and serve. *Negligible carbohydrate.*

MY OWN COLD RHUBARB SOUP

½ pint rhubarb purée not too thick, not too sweet. 4 mint leaves sliced.

A refrigerator is a must for this soup. Half an hour before serving mix in the mint leaves cut with scissors. Return it to the refrigerator and serve in two cups.

The first time I tried this was on a scorching hot day. I had a tumbler-full of thickish rhubarb juice in the refrigerator and didn't know how to use it. It was the 'thin end' so to speak of sieved rhubarb from the day before's rhubarb fool. I tried it as above and it was a most refreshing start to the midday meal. But don't attempt it without a refrigerator. *Negligible carbohydrate.*

ONION SOUP

1 large onion peeled and diced, ½ oz. butter, 1 dessert-spoonful of flour, about a tablespoonful vinegar, 1 pint water, ¼ pint milk, seasoning which should include a pinch of powdered mace. Grated cheese if desired.

Melt the butter in the soup pan. Add the diced onion and toss it well in the butter without letting it discolour. Add the vinegar and leave covered over a gentle heat for about 10 minutes, adding a little water if it gets too dry. Stir in the flour mixed with a pinch of mace and add the water gradually to prevent lumps. Stir until boiling and simmer slowly until the onions are tender, about 30 minutes. Stir in the milk, adjust seasoning and serve with grated cheese if liked. Two servings. *Each serving contains 5 gm. of carbohydrate.*

VEGETABLE MARROW SOUP

8 oz. vegetable marrow weighed after peeling and removing seeds, 1 medium-sized onion peeled and chopped, ½ oz. margarine, 1 teaspoonful flour mixed with a saltspoonful of powdered ginger, 1 pint good stock which can be made from bones of roast meat, salt and pepper. Cream optional.

Melt the margarine in the soup pan. Add the marrow roughly cut along with the onion. Toss all together for a few minutes then sprinkle in the flour. Mix thoroughly, add the stock gradually and stir until boiling. Season to taste and leave to simmer until the marrow is cooked—about 30 minutes. Strain the soup, squashing the marrow through, return all to the rinsed pan, bring to boil and serve. Two servings.

A little cream or milk can be added and, if on a strict diet, omit flour and margarine. A delicious way of serving an insipid vegetable. *Negligible carbohydrate.*

SPINACH SOUP

> *2 tablespoonfuls of sieved spinach, 1 pint white stock or milk and water, salt, pepper and a grating of nutmeg, 2 tablespoonfuls cream.*

Mix spinach and stock together. Bring to boil, season to taste, grating in the nutmeg. Pour the cream in the hot soup cups and whisk while you mix the boiling soup in. Two servings. *Negligible carbohydrate.*

MUSHROOM SOUP

> *½ oz. butter, 1 small onion diced neatly, 4 oz. mushrooms, 1 pint white stock or water, 1 teaspoonful flour, ½ tea-cupful milk, ½ teaspoonful celery salt and seasoning. Cream optional.*

Melt the butter, add the diced onion and toss without discolouring. Add the mushrooms washed, peeled and sliced along with the stalks finely chopped. Cook for a few minutes. Sprinkle in the flour and gradually add the water or stock, blending well in at first to prevent lumps. Bring to boil, add the milk, celery salt and seasoning. Simmer for about 30 minutes and serve. Cream added at the last is also pleasing. Two servings.

About a teaspoonful of caraway seeds can be cooked

with the mushrooms occasionally to give variation. *Each serving contains 5 gm. of carbohydrate.*

CURRIED VEGETABLE SOUP

½ oz. margarine, 1 medium-sized onion, 1 apple, scraps of bayleaf and thyme, 1 teaspoonful of flour mixed with a saltspoonful of curry powder, a small piece turnip, a coarse piece of celery, 2 teaspoonful desiccated coconut, salt, 1 teaspoonful bottled tomato sauce, 2 breakfastcupfuls water and one of milk.

Toss the chopped onion, herbs and apple in the hot margarine and cook without discolouring for a minute or two. Sprinkle in the flour and mix in the water gradually. Bring to boil, add the chopped vegetables, coconut and salt to taste and leave to simmer until the vegetables are tender. Add the tomato sauce towards the end, squash through a strainer, reheat with milk and serve. Two servings. We both enjoyed it. *Each serving contains 10 gm. of carbohydrate.*

FISH SOUP

½ lb. cheap white fish, a small diced onion, a squeeze of lemon, a shaving of lemon rind, 2 breakfastcupfuls water or milk and water, parsley stalks and some freshly chopped parsley, a little anchovy essence if possible and some cream and egg-yolk, if desired, to thicken.

Put the fish, onion, lemon rind and tied parsley stalks in the soup pan along with the liquid. Bring to boil, add lemon juice, season to taste and simmer 20 minutes. Remove the fish and flake it, or sieve, adding a little cream to help it through. Return all but the stalks to the rinsed pan, add a few drops of anchovy, adjust seasoning, bring to boil and serve. If desired thicker, pour the hot soup over a yolk of egg broken with a spoonful of cream, whisking the egg as you pour. Add the chopped parsley last. *This recipe makes 2 servings. If milk is used, each serving contains 5 gm. of carbohydrate.*

LIVER SOUP

4 oz. liver, 2½ breakfastcupfuls water, 1 diced onion, scraps of bayleaf, thyme, salt, pepper and a pinch of ground cloves.

Cook the liver in the water with onion and herbs tied, season to taste. When quite tender, remove the liver and put it through the mincer (fine blade). Return the minced liver to the soup, remove herbs, adjust seasoning along with the cloves and serve hot for two. *Negligible carbohydrate.*

VEGETABLE SOUPS

Vegetable soups such as celery, cauliflower or turnip can be made as follows. Cook them in salted water until tender. Squash through a strainer. Dilute the *purée* with equal quantities of the cooking liquor and milk. Reheat and serve, seasoned with powdered mace, celery salt, or nutmeg and thickened with yolk of egg and cream as directed under Fish Soup. Use only the coarse outside

23

pieces for celery. *Half a teacupful of milk contains 5 gm. of carbohydrate.*

PEANUT SOUP

½ pint each milk and water, 2 rounded dessertspoonfuls of peanut butter, 1 small diced onion, 2 tablespoonfuls finely chopped celery heart, salt, pepper and ½ teaspoonful paprika.

Put all the ingredients except the paprika in the soup pan, bring to boil and simmer about 20 minutes, adding more salt and pepper to taste, with the paprika, just before serving.

This is a lovely soup on a cold day. Frankly I don't think the paprika puts it up or down except for colour, and it could be omitted. *This recipe makes 2 servings. Each serving contains 5 gm. of carbohydrate.*

A NICE SOLE DISH

4 nice fillets of sole, some shredded crabmeat mixed with French dressing (page 67), 1 gill cream mixed with salt, pepper and 2 teaspoonfuls each Worcester Sauce and bottled tomato sauce. Lemon, salt and pepper, and lettuce leaves.

Sprinkle a little lemon juice over the fillets, rub with a little salt and pepper and fold in half or three. Place in a well-buttered dish, cover with buttered paper and bake in gentle oven until tender. Leave to cool.

When quite cold and ready to serve, place each portion in a crisp lettuce leaf, coat with the cream mixture and crown with a portion of crabmeat. Serve well chilled for two. *Negligible carbohydrate*.

MY OWN FISH CREAM

8 oz. chopped cooked fish, 2 oz. chopped potted shrimps, 4 tablespoonfuls of thick cream, about a teaspoonful anchovy essence, salt and freshly ground pepper, ¼ pint jellied fish stock or aspic, 1 stiffly beaten egg-white and cucumber slices in French dressing, or other garnishes as desired. Mayonnaise served separately.

Chop the fish very fine. It must weigh 8 oz. after skin and bone is removed. Mix it with the shrimps, add the cream slightly whipped, anchovy and seasoning. Finally stir in the stock melted but cold and when just setting fold in the stiffly beaten egg-white. Turn into a border or plain mould rinsed with cold water and leave to set. Turn out, garnish it with the cucumber in the centre, or place it round the base in alternate clumps with watercress, radish and lettuce heart. Serve with Mayonnaise (page 67). Four servings. When I make it with plaice I put the fish bones and trimmings in to poach with the fillets and the liquid jells firm enough for my purpose. The liquor from poached turbot makes a sure jelly. *Negligible carbohydrate*.

TURBOT FILLETS BONNEFOY

4 individual-sized pieces of turbot, 4 shallots or 2 small onions, 4 oz. mushrooms, 1 or 2 wineglasses of claret, about ¼ pint well flavoured tomato sauce, a tablespoonful of thick cream, a walnut of butter.

Wash and dry the fish. Dip the pieces lightly in well-seasoned flour and place them in a well-buttered deep dish. Sprinkle the fish with the shallots finely chopped and the mushrooms, washed, peeled and sliced. Add the wine. Cover with well-buttered paper and bake in a slow oven until the fish is tender, 20–30 minutes.

Put the tomato sauce and cream in a saucepan and into it pour the liquor and mushrooms from the cooked fish. Add the butter, let it boil for a minute, adjust the seasoning, pour it over the fish and serve it hot. *This recipe makes 4 servings. Each serving contains negligible carbohydrate.*

OMELET ARNOLD BENNETT

3 eggs, 3 tablespoonfuls of cooked finnan haddock skinned, boned and flaked, 1 tablespoonful cream and the same of cheese mixed with a speck of cayenne, a little seasoning to include grated nutmeg, ¼ pint cheese sauce and some grated cheese for top.

Mix the beaten eggs, fish, cream, cheese and seasoning together and make a nice, lightly set, cushion-shaped omelet. Slide on to a hot fire-proof dish, coat with the cheese sauce, scatter grated cheese on top and brown under the grill. For those on a strict diet the cheese sauce can be omitted. Serves two. *Without cheese sauce, the recipe contains negligible gm. of carbohydrate. Half a teacupful of milk and 1 level dessertspoonful of flour each contain 5 gm.*

JELLIED OR MALAYAN CRAB

1 good-sized crab, 1 tin tomatoes (14 oz.), ½ small chopped onion, 1 clove, ½ oz. gelatine, cream (2 tablespoons), salt and pepper to taste, 1 teaspoonful each of anchovy essence and tarragon vinegar.

Put the tomatoes on to cook with the onion, clove and gelatine. Simmer for about 20 minutes and rub through a sieve. Add 2 tablespoons thin cream, tarragon vinegar and season to taste.

Meanwhile you have taken the meat from the body and claws of the crab and discarded the grey spongy gills. Reserve a little of the flaked claw meat for garnish and stir the rest of the crabmeat into the tomato. Add the anchovy, adjust seasoning and turn into a glass dish. Scatter the garnish over and leave to set. Serve as cold as possible. Two greedy servings and it is really good.

The crabmeat comes to about 6 oz. Some of this could be run into a picnic carton to use as a packed meal. *Each serving contains 5 gm. of carbohydrate.*

MUTTON CUTLETS IN TOMATO ASPIC
(Mrs. Colville)

3 cooked mutton cutlets, ½ pint liquid aspic or dissolve ½ oz. gelatine in ½ pint tasty stock, ½ pint liquid from tinned tomatoes, a tablespoonful of bottled tomato sauce, seasoning.

The cutlets should be from best end or loin. Cut them through at the joint and trim them taking them right off the bone if necessary.

Mix the aspic, tomato liquid and bottled sauce together. Taste for seasoning and add if desired a speck of Worcester sauce. Stir occasionally and when nearly setting pour it over the cutlets. When set, garnish with vegetable salad and some of the salvaged tinned tomatoes. Lovely.

When I do this I buy a piece of loin of lamb (about 2½ lb.) braise it in the piece and have it hot the first day, keeping the best cutlets back as cold for the aspic. Two cutlets set in a picnic carton would make a nice packed meal. *This recipe makes 3 servings. Each serving contains negligible carbohydrate.*

MEAT CAKES

12 oz. raw lean beef cut from the aitchbone or similar lean cut, a small cooked potato (2 oz.), about half a medium-sized raw onion, a slice Ryvita, 1 egg, seasoning, stock.

Put the meat through the mincer using the finest blade. I use the Ryvita and onion by degrees to help the meat through as it gets a bit pulpy. Put the potato through as well. Mix in the egg which need not be beaten and add the seasoning. Form into four cakes. Dip in a little seasoned flour and fry brown on both sides. Pour off surplus fat (leaving the cakes in the pan), add tasty stock to come half-way up the cakes, cover with a lid and leave to cook slowly for about 30 minutes turning them during the process. Serve hot for two; and they are good cold for anyone who has to carry a meal. *Each serving contains 5 gm. of carbohydrate.*

MY OWN MEAT PUDDING

8 oz. stewing steak weighed free of gristle and fat, 2 oz. raw bacon, 1 medium-sized onion, 1 tablespoon raw rice, 2 eggs, seasoning. Brown sauce or Tomato sauce.

Put meat, bacon and onion through the mincer using the medium blade. Add the rice, seasoning and beaten egg and mix well. Turn into a well-greased pudding basin and steam gently for 3 hours. Turn carefully out and coat with rich brown or tomato sauce. Four servings. *Each serving contains 5 gm. of carbohydrate.*

BEEF FARCI

About 1¾ lb. stewing steak cut in one piece and a good inch thick, 4 oz. lean pork, 4 oz. pork fat, 1 onion or 2 shallots, salt and 2 pinches of mixed spice, 2 or 3 rashers streaky bacon, ½ pint water, 1 wineglass of dry white wine, 2 tablespoonfuls tomato ketchup, some slices of carrot, 1 large chopped onion, a grating of nutmeg, a little lard and a few bones or a chicken carcass.

Put the pork (lean and fat) through the mincer along with the shallots. Mix it well together by hand, season with salt and mixed spice.

Cut the steak through the middle to within about an ⅛ in. of the other end and open it out like a book. Sprinkle a little salt over each side and spread the bottom side with the pork mixture, making it smooth and even. On this place the rashers without rind and replace the top. Stitch the open end down with thick cotton and leave a good length so that it can be easily pulled out at serving time. Tie the steak across with clean string in three places and also lengthways.

Melt a spoonful of pure lard in the saucepan and when hot brown the meat quickly in it on both sides. Pour away surplus fat, add the water and bring to boil. Add the carrot and onion mixed with the nutmeg, the white wine and bones with salt to taste and leave to cook (covered) very slowly for about 3 hours, or until steak is tender when probed with a skewer. Add the ketchup about an hour before the end. Leave to get quite cold in the saucepan and press it a little if necessary but not until it is cold.

To serve, remove the solid fat and string and glaze with some of the gravy which can be fortified with a little gelatine if necessary. Four to six servings.

This is truly lovely food—rich and satisfying and well worth the trouble to prepare, but don't cheese-pare on the wine—it makes the dish and is necessary to counteract the richness.

Slices of this would be excellent for a packed meal. *Each slice contains negligible carbohydrate.*

ROAST OX HEART

2½ lb. ox heart and some veal or sage and onion stuffing, seasoning and some dripping.

This will be nearly a whole heart. Wash it thoroughly, removing the blood and gristle, and dry. Pop the stuffing into the cavities, tie up if necessary and rub pepper and salt over.

Take a sheet of greaseproof large enough to envelop the heart and spread it generously with dripping. Parcel the heart in it, place it in a roasting tin and put it in the oven at 400 deg. Leave at this temperature for about 15 minutes, then switch back to 300 deg. and leave to cook for 2½–3 hours. About 15 minutes before the end, remove the paper, baste the heart and return it to the oven to brown. Serve with good brown gravy. Something my husband is very fond of. The heart done like this (*en papillote*) is tender and moist and needs no basting while cooking; so you can safely leave it to its own devices while you do your morning's shopping. *Negligible carbohydrate.*

HARICOT OF OX TAIL

Wash the tail and cut through at the joints. Put it on to boil in cold water barely to cover, with a little salt. When boiling point is reached, pour away the water and trim excess fat from the joints, if any. Roll the pieces in seasoned flour and fry them in hot dripping. Remove them from the fat, add some diced mixed vegetables such as carrot, onion, and celery along with a level teaspoonful of powdered mixed herbs and about two cubed rashers of streaky bacon. Fry these lightly in the fat, replace the tail and add water just to cover. Bring to the boil, season to taste and leave to simmer until tender, 3–4 hours. Skim off fat and serve hot. Some tomato *purée* and a few drops of Worcester sauce may be added. *Negligible carbohydrate.*

CALF'S HEAD

Put the brains to soak in a basin of cold salted water . Scrape the bloody bits from the head and put it to soak overnight in cold salted water. The following day wash the head well under cold water and put in a pan with cold water to cover. Bring to boil and pour off the water. Cover in more cold water, bring to boil, add salt to taste and simmer until the meat is tender 2–3 hours—they vary in time. While the head cooks add half a lemon from which the juice has been extracted, a good bunch of washed parsley, carrot, onion, a bayleaf and sprig of thyme.

I finish the head this way; scrape the meat from the bones, skin and slice the tongue. Put the tongue and half the meat on to a hot serving dish, coat with onion sauce and serve at once. Two servings.

The rest of the meat I put in a small basin along with the brains (cooked and diced), seasoned with grated nutmeg or powdered mace and filled with stock from the head which should jelly when cold. Two servings.

To cook the brains. Rinse them, put them on in cold water and bring to boil. Pour off the water and simmer them in fresh water with salt to taste for 20 minutes or until tender. The brains can be broken up and added to white sauce, scrambled egg or omelet. *Negligible carbohydrate.*

ONION SAUCE

1 good-sized onion, 1 tablespoon margarine and 1 level tablespoon of flour, about ½ pint stock from the head, seasoning to include, if possible, a suspicion of powdered mace.

Melt the margarine. Add the onion, peeled and chopped, along with 2 tablespoonfuls of the stock. Leave to cook gently (covered) for about 10 minutes when the onion should be nearly tender. Stir in the flour, mixing it well to get it lump free, add the rest of the stock gradually at first and stir until boiling. Simmer 8–10 minutes. Adjust seasoning and serve. *This recipe contains 15 gm. of carbohydrate.*

ALMOND-OLIVE SAUCE

1 tablespoonful margarine, 1 crushed clove garlic, 4 tomatoes skinned and chopped, 8 olives stoned and chopped, 12 almonds blanched and shredded, a bayleaf, ¼ pint stock, a tablespoonful of freshly chopped parsley and seasoning.

Cook the garlic, tomatoes, olives, almonds and bayleaf in the hot margarine for about 10 minutes, stirring often and keeping the heat low to prevent sticking. Season to taste, add the stock and simmer for a minute or two. Remove the bayleaf, stir in the freshly chopped parsley, season and serve.

This is also a good sauce to serve with calf's head. Delicious too with hot boiled tongue or game casserole. *Negligible carbohydrate.*

DEVONSHIRE PORK PIE

1 *lb. pork, 2 medium-sized apples, peeled, cored and sliced, 1 nice-sized chopped onion, ½ teaspoonful of powdered sage, seasoning, and thinly rolled flaky pastry made from 4 oz. flour.*

Choose fairly lean pork and cut in neat pieces. Sprinkle with a little salt and pepper. Mix the sage with the onion and put the pork, apple and onion in the pie dish with water to barely cover. Top with the pastry and bake in a moderate oven 350 deg. lessening to 300 deg. until the pork is cooked, about 2 hours. Serve hot. Don't remove too much fat as the pie needs a little. It could of course be cooked *en casserole* for those who can't eat pastry. *This recipe makes 4 servings. Each serving contains 25 gm. of carbohydrate.*

VEAL LOAF

12 *oz. veal, ¼ lb. ham, 1 oz. breadcrumbs, ¼ teaspoonful of powdered mixed herbs, 1 egg, salt and pepper.*

Mince the veal and the ham. Add the crumbs, seasoning, herbs and beaten egg and mix well together. Turn into a small greased loaf tin, cover with greased paper and bake in a slow oven 300 deg. for 2 hours. Leave in the tin to cool and serve cold. I stand the tin in a roasting-tin of water while cooking. This is a delicious standby for cold food or a packed meal. Six servings.

Once when I had no powdered herbs I put the tip of a bay leaf and a very tiny sprig of thyme through with the meat, grated less than quarter of a lemon on the fine grater and followed it with a grating of nutmeg. *Negligible carbohydrate.*

CHILE CON CARNE

½ lb. beef steak, 1 small tin Vienna sausages, 1 large onion, 1 teaspoonful or more curry powder, 1 medium-sized tin tomatoes and some runner beans, along with salt and pepper.

Mince the steak and fry with the chopped onion until light brown. Add the sausages, cut in small pieces, along with the rest of the ingredients. Simmer slowly for about an hour. I do this dish when there are plenty of runner beans about. Cook them separately and add them at the last. Two good servings. *Each serving contains 5 gm. of carbohydrate.*

THE END OF AN OLD SONG

4 oz. minced cooked belly pork, 2 oz. mashed potatoes, 1 small raw onion, seasoning to taste and a beaten egg.

As belly pork is very fat, cut away the surplus and use the meat as lean as possible. Mix in the potato, minced onion, seasoning and egg. Form into cakes (three) and fry on both sides, or spoon the mixture into hot fat. Useful for a packed meal; and boiled pork can go on and *on* if something isn't done about it. *The 3 cakes contain 10 gm. of carbohydrate.*

Savoury Food

CORNED BEEF RISSOLES

1 tin corned beef (12 oz.), 4 oz. mashed potato, 1 small raw onion, 1 egg, salt and pepper.

Put the beef and onion through the mincer. Add the potato, drop in the egg and mix thoroughly. Season to taste and form into rissoles. Roll in very little flour to give a smooth coating and fry in smoking hot deep fat until golden. Drain on soft paper and serve hot for tea, or cold for a packed meal. Makes six good-sized rissoles. *Two rissoles contain 5 gm. of carbohydrate.*

STUFFED MARROW

½ medium-sized marrow cut through cross-ways. 8 oz. cooked meat, 2 rashers bacon, 1 medium-sized onion, 1 egg, salt and pepper and a little anchovy essence if possible.

Mince the meat, bacon and onion. Add the egg and seasoning and mix well.

Peel the marrow, carefully scoop out the seeds and boil it in salted water for about 5 minutes. Drain *thoroughly*. Fill the cavity with the meat and cover the top with a cabbage leaf or some buttered paper. Tie it down and roast in hot dripping at 400 deg. for 30–40 minutes. Serve hot, cut in circles, with tasty gravy. Two greedy portions.

Raw minced beef, of course, can be used instead of cooked, or such a mixture as is given under veal loaf; but allow longer time for roasting. It is, however, a nice way of using up cold meat and a *change. Negligible carbohydrate.*

STUFFED CABBAGE

1 *medium-sized cabbage weighing not less than* 8 *oz., filling as for stuffed marrow, stock as required, seasoning.*

Trim very bruised outside leaves from the cabbage and cut the stalk level so that it sits evenly. Wash it and bring it to the boil in cold salted water. Drain it from the water and pour the water away. The leaves should now open out like a flower, so inspect them carefully for creepy-crawlies. Pack the filling into the cabbage, gather the cabbage into shape again and tie round the centre with cotton. I sometimes fit a paper-clip right on top to secure the tip. Place in a saucepan with the stock, sprinkle a little salt over and simmer gently (covered) for about an hour, or until the leaves are tender. Or cook in the oven *en casserole*. Whole potatoes can be dropped in and cooked in the stock thus saving fuel and labour. A good way of using up a tired bit of ham. *Negligible carbohydrate.*

STUFFED ONIONS

Choose good-sized onions of a nice shape. Parboil them whole in salted water to taste and drain *thoroughly*. Remove the centre parts and stuff the cavity with minced meat as for stuffed vegetable marrow. Cook in stock as for stuffed cabbage. *One large onion contains* 5 *gm. of carbohydrate.*

DOLMAR—STUFFED CABBAGE LEAVES

Choose large well washed cabbage leaves allowing 2 or 3 per person. For filling use either the mixture given under My Own Meat Pudding or the one for Veal Loaf.

Put the leaves on to boil in cold salted water. When boiling point is reached, strain them. They should now be soft and pliable. Dry them and divide the mixture among them placing a tidy roll of it on each leaf. Roll the leaves up and tie them securely, length and breadthways, so that no filling escapes. Fry the rolls lightly in a little hot fat, pour off surplus fat, add stock barely to cover and simmer for 1½–2 hours. *See respective stuffings for figures.*

KIDNEY FLAMBÉ

Split open (but not through) some sheep's or lamb's kidneys. Remove the skin along with the fat core, wash and dry. Dip them lightly in a little flour nicely seasoned with pepper and salt. Then fry lightly or grill them, keeping them underdone or they will toughen. When ready have them all together in the pan, pour over them 1 or 2 tablespoonfuls of brandy and set it alight. Leave it to burn, then serve the kidneys on hot buttered toast. Pour a little hot water in the pan, mix it well until boiling to incorporate the delectable kidney essence, and serve it with the kidneys. *One slice of large thinly-sliced cut-loaf contains 15 gm. of carbohydrate.*

Savoury Food

SCOTCH EGGS

3 small hard-boiled eggs, 4 oz. cooked beef, 2 oz. raw bacon rashers (free of rind,) a suspicion of raw onion (optional), seasoning and a beaten egg.

Mince the beef, bacon and onion together. Add beaten egg and seasoning. Mix thoroughly. Divide the meat into three equal portions and wrap a shelled egg in each—best done with wet hands. Smooth all joints to get an even coating, roll very lightly in flour and fry in smoking hot deep fat until golden. Drain in soft paper, cut in half and serve with good gravy. These could be coated with the veal loaf mixture. They make an excellent packed meal. *Negligible carbohydrate.*

STUFFED EGGS

3 hard-boiled eggs, 2 oz. cooked mushrooms—about 5 or 6, ½ oz. butter, salt and pepper.

Cut a shaving of the white from each egg so that it sits evenly and also cut out a small circle so that you can scoop out the yolk without breaking the white. Press the yolks through a strainer along with the butter and mix to a smooth paste. Add salt to taste, plenty of freshly ground pepper and the mushroom caps cut in neat dice. Season highly and pack the mixture back into the whites heaping it well on top. Serve on crisp lettuce garnished with sprigs of watercress and julienne of tomato tossed in French dressing (page 66). For a pretty-pretty effect the eggs can be glazed with liquid aspic almost at setting point.

Other suggested fillings for stuffed eggs. After sieving add about a teaspoonful of anchovy essence and enough Worcester sauce to make it really tasty, or work in a little curry powder, or some minced ham, chicken or tongue. Sardines can be added but they should be sieved (skinned and boned) with the yolks. At all costs season the mixture highly, otherwise the result will be tasteless.

Stuffed eggs make a good packed meal, for hard-boiled eggs are stodgy and dull. For a carried lunch fill the eggs only level, replace the lid and wrap them in a lettuce leaf. *Negligible carbohydrate.*

EGG CUTLETS

3 hard-boiled eggs, 3 oz. mashed potatoes, 1 beaten egg, freshly chopped parsley, 2 oz. chopped cooked mushrooms or 1 oz. shrimps, with anchovy essence or Worcester sauce to flavour.

Chop the eggs finely. Mix with the potato and mushrooms, work in the beaten egg, add parsley and season nicely. Form into cutlets or patties, roll lightly in flour and fry golden in smoking hot deep fat. Makes four. If shrimps are added, season with a teaspoonful of anchovy essence and a grating of nutmeg. If a large egg is used the mixture can be very soft but it will at least form into cakes. Good hot, or cold for a packed meal. *Each patty contains 5 gm. of carbohydrate.*

EGG MOUSSE

4 hard-boiled eggs, ½ pint cream, 3 tablespoonfuls of melted stiff aspic, Worcester, tomato or anchovy sauce to taste, salt and pepper to taste, with dressed cucumber slices, etc., and aspic for garnish.

Sieve the yolks and chop the whites very fine on clean greaseproof paper. Half whip the cream. Mix the pounded yolks, flavouring and seasoning together. Stir in the liquid aspic which should be quite cold, then the cream and chopped whites. Adjust the seasoning, stir well and pour into a glass dish to set. When set, surround the edge with wafer-thin slices of cucumber tossed in French dressing, sprinkle a little red pepper, finely chopped parsley or tarragon leaves in the centre and glaze all with aspic at setting point. Four to six servings.

This is obviously a party dish, but easily made and superb. *Negligible carbohydrate.*

PIPERADE

1 green or red pepper or use a tinned pimiento, 1 large onion, 4 large tomatoes or use 6 tinned tomatoes, 1 small (very small) level teaspoonful of curry powder, a touch of garlic, 3 eggs, 1 oz. butter, a teaspoonful olive oil and seasoning.

Melt the butter and oil and when hot add the chopped pepper and leave to cook (covered) until tender—about

20 minutes. Add the onion finely chopped and cook for a further 10 minutes, then add the sliced tomatoes without skin and pips along with the garlic-clove and curry powder. Season to taste and cook gently until all is a nice *purée*—a further 5–10 minutes. Remove the pan from the heat and beat in the eggs quickly, one at a time and whole. Return the mixture to the heat and stir continually until quite hot but not boiling. Two servings—makes a nice change for high tea. *Each serving contains 5 gm. of carbohydrate.*

FISH OMELET SOUFFLÉ
(Economical)

4 oz. cooked flaked fish, 3 eggs, salt, pepper, lard to prepare the pan, and about ½ oz. butter.

Beat a whole egg and two yolks together. Add the flaked fish, free of skin and bone along with salt and pepper. Finally fold in the stiffly beaten egg-whites.

Melt a little lard in the omelet pan, make it quite hot, swill it round then pour it away. Now throw in the butter and when hot pour in the fish mixture. Leave it to cook for about 2 minutes, or until the bottom is set and brown. Place the pan in a hot oven (450 deg.) until set, 6–8 minutes. Make a small slit in the centre, fold the omelet over and serve. Two huge portions. Nice, needs plenty of pepper. Smoked fish, ham, tongue or chicken could be substituted for fish. *Negligible carbohydrate.*

Savoury Food

OUR OWN CURRIED EGGS

3 soft-boiled eggs, 1 oz. margarine, 1 rounded tablespoon-ful of flour mixed with less than a level teaspoonful of curry powder, ¾ pint milk and seasoning.

First make a white sauce with the margarine, flour, curry and the milk. Leave to simmer 8 minutes and season to taste.

Boil the eggs for 3½ minutes, run them under cold water and shell them carefully. When the sauce has simmered long enough, drop in the eggs whole and with a sharp spoon cut them roughly into the sauce. Now put the pan on a gentle heat again and stir all together for a moment or two but do not let it boil. Serve hot for two.

This is something we both like. Adding the eggs soft and breaking them into the sauce gives all a velvety texture and *not* leathery eggs. *One serving contains 20 gm. of carbohydrate.*

EGGS SOUBISE

1 good-sized cooking onion, 1 oz. butter or margarine, ½ oz. flour, ¼ pint milk, 3 or 4 eggs, salt and pepper, a spoonful or two of cream or milk-top and about 1 oz. grated cheese for top.

Cook the diced onion in the hot butter for about 15 minutes. Do not let it discolour and stir it occasionally. Stir in the flour and gradually add the milk. Stir until boiling and simmer 8–10 minutes. Pour the sauce into a flat buttered fire-proof dish and over it break the eggs whole. Scatter a little salt and freshly milled pepper over, cover with the cream and grated cheese which can have a whiff of cayenne incorporated and bake in a moderate oven (350 deg.) for about 15 minutes, when the eggs should be lightly set. If not brown stand it under the grill for a minute. Lovely! A little freshly grated nutmeg, celery salt, or powdered mace could be added occasionally to the onions to give a subtle flavour. *This recipe makes 2 servings. Each serving contains 10 gm. of carbohydrate.*

EGG PATTIES

Line individual patty tins with short pastry thinly rolled. Strew the bottoms with chopped fried bacon rashers. Drop a raw egg in each pastry case, dust with salt and pepper then strew each egg with some more chopped bacon. Cover with a lid of thin pastry, crimp the edges well together, brush with milk and egg mixed and bake in a moderate oven until the pastry is golden and cooked. Make two slits on each patty when you remove them from the oven. Serve hot or cold. Handy for a packed meal. Some fried onion could be mixed with the bacon. *Quarter of an oz. of pastry (baked or unbaked) contains 5 gm. of carbohydrate.*

AN EGG DISH OF MY OWN

2 small onions, about a dessertspoonful of finely chopped sage, about a tablespoonful of margarine, 3 beaten eggs, ½ pint milk, salt and pepper, a little grated cheese for top.

I do this on the grill-plate in a covered Pyrex as it saves

putting on the oven. Make the margarine hot and in it cook the sliced onions mixed with the sage and a little salt and pepper. Cover the dish and leave to cook on top of the grill-plate, turning the onions over frequently and adding more margarine if necessary. They should not get brown, merely let them sweat in the fat until tender—10–15 minutes.

Add the milk to the eggs, season to taste and when the onions are cooked, pour the custard slowly over. Replace the lid and leave to cook slowly, turning the grill-plate to 'low' if necessary. Leave until almost set, then cover the top with grated cheese. Switch the grill to 'high' and stand the dish under the grill until lightly set and evenly brown. Good: enough for three. *Each serving contains 5 gm. of carbohydrate.*

EGG AND CRESS PIE

Scraps of short pastry rolled thin. 2 oz. margarine, 2 oz. bunch watercress, 4 eggs, salt and pepper.

Line a 9-in. greased Pyrex plate with short pastry rolled wafer thin. Soften the margarine and work into it the chopped watercress, discarding the very coarse stems. Spread half the paste over the pastry, break the eggs whole on this and season them. Put the rest of the watercress paste in blobs here and there—it just won't sit on the eggs. Wet the pastry edge and cover with a pastry lid of transparent thinness. Crimp the edges and bake in a moderately hot oven 375 deg. F. for about 25 minutes, when the pastry should be cooked. Remove from the oven and make four small slits on the pastry to let steam escape. This has a spinachy taste and it would make a good

packed meal. 4 oz. short pastry would be more than
ample for this dish for the pastry must be thin, thin. *Quarter
of an oz. of pastry contains 5 gm. of carbohydrate.*

SARDINES PIEDMONTAISE

1 *tin sardines,* 2 *large eggs,* ½ *teaspoonful tarragon
vinegar,* ½ *teaspoonful malt or wine vinegar,* ¼ *teaspoonful
made mustard, salt and pepper and* ½ *oz. butter or
margarine.*

Drain the sardines free of oil and heat them in a fire-proof
dish on top of the grill-plate.

Melt the butter in a small pan. Add vinegars, mustard
and seasonings to the eggs and beat well. Stir them into
the melted butter and keep stirring them over a gentle
heat until creamy. Pour them on the sardines and serve at
once. Surplus oil in the dish must be poured off before
coating with the eggs. Serves two. A pleasant way with
sardines. *Negligible carbohydrate.*

MY OWN SARDINE DISH

1 *or* 2 *tender young cabbages,* 1 *tin sardines in tomato, a
walnut of butter, salt, freshly ground pepper, a grating of
nutmeg,* 2 *oz. grated cheese mixed with a pinch of cayenne.*

Cook the chopped cabbage in a little boiling water until
barely tender. Drain *thoroughly* and toss it in the hot
butter. Season nicely, adding a grating of nutmeg. Turn it
into a well-buttered shallow fire-proof dish, place the
sardines on top along with the tomato sauce and scatter

the cheese over all. Stand under the grill until a crust forms on top. Enough for two. *Negligible carbohydrate*.

CHEESE AIGRETTES

1 oz. margarine, 1 oz. flour, ¼ pint cold water, 4 oz. grated cheese mixed with a snuff of cayenne, salt, a good pinch of dry mustard, 2 eggs separated and deep fat for frying.

Melt the margarine, stir in the flour and add the water gradually, away from the heat. Stir vigorously over a gentle heat until the mixture boils. Cook it until it forms a ball—2 or 3 minutes. Remove from the heat, stir in the flavoured cheese and the yolks. Add salt to taste and finally stir in the stiffly beaten whites. Drop dessertspoonfuls of the mixture into smoking hot deep fat and fry until golden, turning them gently in the process. Makes 12 or 14. They have a delicate protective shell holding curdy cheese within and are so good that two will eat the lot. *This recipe contains 20 gm. of carbohydrate.*

CHEESE PUDDING

2 oz. slice bread including the crust, 4½ oz. grated cheese mixed with pinches of cayenne, dry mustard and a little salt, 2 small eggs beaten, ½ pint milk.

Put the milk on to boil. Dice the bread and mix it in a basin with the cheese, reserving the odd ½ oz. for the top. Pour the boiling milk over and leave to soak for 15

47

minutes. Stir in the well-beaten eggs and pour into a buttered pie dish. Scatter what is left of the grated cheese on top and bake at 375 deg., mark 5, for 25 minutes or until brown and set. More than enough for two but we eat it and spend the rest of the evening repenting of our greed! *Each serving contains 20 gm. of carbohydrate.*

COOKED CHEESE

6 oz. grated cheese mixed with 1 oz. flour, a good pinch of salt, dry mustard and cayenne, ½ pint milk (scant measure), toast.

Put the cheese, flour and seasoning well mixed in a saucepan. Stir in the milk and cook over a steady heat until boiling, stirring continually. Simmer for 10 minutes then leave to thicken for a few minutes on a warm part of the stove but not over direct heat. Serve hot on toast. D.'s favourite for tea. *This recipe makes 2 servings. Each serving (without toast) contains 15 gm. of carbohydrate. One oz. of bread toasted contains 15 gm. of carbohydrate.*

CHEESE FINGERS

Make as above but reduce milk to about 7 oz. to get a thickish sauce. Remove from the heat, stir in two yolks or a well-beaten egg. Turn into a flat dish and leave to cool. When quite cold, cut into fingers and fry. *See above for carbohydrate figures.*

CHEESE SOUFFLÉ

Use quantities as for cheese fingers and make as above but add 2 yolks when removed from the heat and fold in the whites, stiffly beaten. Turn into a greased *soufflé* dish, round which a band of greased paper is tied to come above the rim. Bake in a hot oven (400 deg. F.) for 25 minutes when it should be risen, golden in colour and lightly set. Serve at once in a folded napkin and without the band. Stand the dish in a tin of water while baking. *This recipe makes 2 servings. Each serving contains 15 gm. of carbohydrate.*

CHEESEY EGGS

Break as many eggs (whole) as you require into a flat well-buttered fire-proof dish. Spoon a little cream, or milk-top over and some seasoning. Cover them with a hefty layer of grated cheese tinctured with a spot of cayenne and bake in a hot oven until set. Good, too, baked in individual ramekin dishes. If the oven isn't on, start them on top of the grill-plate and brown them underneath but don't get them leathery. *Negligible carbohydrate.*

SWISS EGGS

Put slices of Gruyère cheese and skinned tomato in a buttered fire-proof dish. Break the eggs over and finish as above. *Negligible carbohydrate.*

CHEESE CUSTARD

3 eggs, 4–6 oz. grated cheese mixed with pinches of salt, cayenne and dry mustard and ½ pint milk.

Beat the eggs, mix in most of the cheese and the milk. Turn into a greased pie dish, scatter the rest of the grated cheese on top and bake at 350 deg. F., until set. *This recipe makes 2 servings. Each serving contains 5 gm. of carbohydrate.*

CHEESE CUSTARD PIE

Make as above and turn into a shallow dish lined with short pastry thinly rolled. Scatter grated cheese on top and bake as for custard pie. Good for a packed meal. *Quarter of an oz. of pastry contains 5 gm. of carbohydrate.*

WELSH RAREBIT

4 oz. stale well-flavoured cheddar, mixed with pinches of salt, cayenne and dry mustard, 2 tablespoons beer, a beaten egg and toast fingers.

Put the grated cheese in a small pan, make a well in the centre and pour in the beer. Heat the mixture slowly and stir until the cheese is melted. Mix in the beaten egg and stir until it thickens but does not boil. Serve hot. It should be eaten with fingers of toast. Enough for one. *Half an oz. of toast contains 10 gm. of carbohydrate.*

Savoury Food

EGGS IN JELLY

1 medium-sized tin of consommé, 1 rounded teaspoonful of gelatine, 1 egg per person, some double cream, salt and pepper and Worcester sauce if required.

Poach very lightly 1 egg per person and slip them into a dish of cold water.

Dissolve the gelatine over heat and stir into the consommé, warming the consommé a little if desired. Have ready as many individual egg dishes as you have eggs and run a little of the consommé into each one. Leave this to set. Run some more consommé into a separate dish and leave that until almost setting.

Drain the cold eggs thoroughly on a clean cloth, trim them neatly and place them in the prepared dishes. Whip the cream (about ½ gill for 4 eggs) until fairly thick and stir in the consommé when it is almost setting. Taste for seasoning and add a little Worcester sauce if desired. Spoon the mixture over the eggs. Place them quickly in the 'fridge' and finally run a little more of the consommé at setting point over each egg. A delightful dish so long as you don't poach the eggs bullet hard. *Each serving contains negligible gm. of carbohydrate.*

Vegetables

Green vegetables and salads are an essential part of a diabetic's diet. They can be eaten *ad lib.*, so they are useful fillers. As the basic method of preparation and cooking of all vegetables has been fully dealt with in many other books I will but give here suggestions for adding flavour and variety to those in common use. Personally I think the less vegetables are 'messed about' with in cooking the better. Elaborately cooked vegetables can disguise the fact that the initial basic cooking has spoilt them. Thus will they be shorn of much food value, particularly if they have a prolonged second cooking.

VEGETABLE MARROW

Boil or steam some chunks of vegetable marrow until barely tender. Drain *thoroughly*. Melt 1 oz. butter in a saucepan, add a small onion very finely chopped and cook, without discolouring, for 1 minute. Add the marrow along with a good pinch of curry powder, toss all together for a moment or two and serve. Liked even by me. *Negligible carbohydrate*.

MINTED MARROW

Treat the marrow as above but substitute a dessertspoonful of freshly chopped mint for the curry powder. *Negligible carbohydrate*.

FRENCH BEANS LANDAISE

Lightly fry some sliced onion and chopped bacon together. Add the well-drained cooked beans and toss together for a moment or two. Add a turn of the pepper mill and serve. Beans, these days, seem to need a terrific amount of salt to bring out the flavour. *Negligible carbohydrate*.

BEANS ORIENTAL

Boil and drain thoroughly some French or runner beans. Toss them in hot butter and add good pinches of curry powder, ground ginger or a little cinnamon—not too much, just enough to leave one guessing. *Negligible carbohydrate*.

TO SALT BEANS

If you have too many beans coming on at once in your garden, salt them. They can be gathered and salted each day, for only young tender beans should be salted.

Proportions for salting are about 1 lb. cooking salt to 3 lb. beans. String and slice clean beans—it is better not to wash them as they get washed well before cooking. Put a ¼-in. layer of salt and one of sliced beans in a jar or crock and continue alternately until the beans are used, making the top layer one of salt. Tie down with several layers of greaseproof. They will be most welcome when vegetables are scarce and dear. *Negligible carbohydrate*.

TO COOK SALT BEANS

Remove as many beans as you require and wash them six times in cold water. Soak them in fairly hot water and leave for about 2 hours. Drain off the water and rinse under fresh cold water. Taste one and if it is still too salt put the beans on in cold water, bring to boil and pour off the water. Drain, then cover in boiling water and boil till tender, tasting the water for you may even have to add salt. Drain *thoroughly* and finish in any of the ways suggested previously.

Don't throw away the salt or brine from the bean jar. I use it instead of ordinary salted water for cooking potatoes and vegetables. *Negligible carbohydrate*.

TO COOK SPINACH

Throw away discoloured leaves and coarse stems. Wash it well to remove grit, so hold the leaves under running water, or soak in a large basin with plenty of water. Give a good stir up and leave for at least 20 minutes, when the grit will settle. Carefully remove the leaves into fresh water and leave as before. Repeat until the water is free of grit.

To cook, put it in a large saucepan containing about an inch of water to which salt and a wee pinch of sugar have been added. Cover with a lid and leave to cook fast until the leaves are tender, though still firm when bruised between finger and thumb. Time varies (young garden-picked spinach should cook inside 5 minutes), so test often and give the spinach a good stir up shortly after you have put it in the pan, to get top leaves to bottom, so to speak. Spinach shrinks a lot in cooking so you'll need masses, even for two. When cooked, drain through a colander and leave for several minutes to let the moisture seep through. Press between two plates and serve in its round shape cut in wedges. This method is called *en branche*. Or finish in any of the following ways. Some people prefer to put the spinach in the pan without water, for it will make its own juice along with what water clings to the leaves. *Negligible carbohydrate.*

SAVOURY SPINACH

Dice 4 rashers of streaky bacon, add a good tablespoonful of finely chopped onion and fry together until crisp. Add well-drained cooked spinach, make thoroughly hot, season nicely and serve. *Negligible carbohydrate.*

SPINACH WITH BLUE CHEESE

Mix an ounce each of blue cheese and butter together. Have ready 2 breakfastcupfuls of spinach *purée*, fresh or tinned, and mix the cheese paste into it. Make thoroughly hot and serve. *Negligible carbohydrate.*

CREAMED SPINACH

Sieve some cooked spinach while hot. Mix the *purée* with a walnut of butter and 1 or 2 tablespoonfuls of cream. Season with freshly ground pepper, a grating of nutmeg and serve. *Negligible carbohydrate.*

SPINACH AU GRATIN

Put some creamed spinach in a buttered fire-proof dish, scatter a good layer of grated cheese on top and brown under the grill.

Creamed spinach is a natural partner to poached and soft-boiled eggs as well as fillets of poached fish, for it is the basis of the classic Florentine dishes. *Negligible carbohydrate.*

SPINACH PIEDMONTAISE

Chop some well-drained cooked spinach. Melt 1 or 2 oz. butter (according to the amount of spinach) in a saucepan. Add 4 anchovy fillets roughly chopped along with about ½-clove garlic crushed. Fry lightly, add the spinach, toss all together until thoroughly hot, adjust seasoning and serve. *Negligible carbohydrate.*

CAULIFLOWER HARLEQUIN

Have ready a cooked, well-drained cauliflower which can be left whole or cut in sprigs.

For the dressing you require 1 hard-boiled egg, a slice of cold ham, 2 oz. melted butter and seasoning.

Chop the egg and dice the ham. Have the butter hot in a small saucepan, put in the other ingredients, season with salt and freshly milled pepper to taste and pour over the cauliflower which should be kept hot in the serving dish. *Negligible carbohydrate.*

CURRIED CAULIFLOWER

Cook ½ diced apple along with ½ diced small onion in a tablespoonful butter and ½ teaspoonful curry powder. When these are tender stir in 4 tablespoonfuls milk-top, season to taste, bring to boil and pour it over the cauliflower. Serve hot. *This recipe makes 2 servings. Each serving contains 5 gm. of carbohydrate.*

CAULIFLOWER WITH TARRAGON SAUCE

Place the hot well-drained cooked cauliflower in the serving dish and coat with hot cream seasoned wistfully with a little tarragon vinegar, salt and pepper. *Negligible carbohydrate.*

CAULIFLOWER AU GRATIN

This can be no more than the cooked cauliflower coated with grated cheese (mixed with pinches of cayenne and dry mustard) and browned under the grill, or it can be further coated with cream and finished as above. But D. insists on having it coated with a thick flour-based cheese sauce. He loves it for tea. *Without flour, this recipe contains negligible gm. of carbohydrate. One level tablespoonful of flour equals 10 gm.*

CABBAGE WITH CARAWAY

Toss the chopped cabbage (after cooking and thorough draining) in a little hot butter or margarine along with ½–1 teaspoonful caraway seeds and some freshly milled pepper. *Negligible carbohydrate.*

CABBAGE WITH HORSE-RADISH

Finish as above but substitute some freshly grated horse-radish or some horse-radish relish for the caraway. *Negligible carbohydrate.*

CABBAGE AND CELERY

When celery is in season cook a small piece of celery heart with the cabbage, it gives a nice flavour—or sprinkle in a little celery salt at the final tossing in butter. *Negligible carbohydrate.*

CABBAGE AU GRATIN

Toss some freshly cooked and *thoroughly* drained chopped cabbage in hot butter and cream—enough to moisten. Season highly, turn into a buttered flat dish, scatter grated cheese over and brown quickly under the grill. Serve hot.

Cabbage is also good with cream sharpened with a little vinegar (tarragon for choice) mixed into it. *Negligible carbohydrate.*

BRUSSELS SPROUTS WITH CHESTNUTS

Boil the sprouts, drain thoroughly and keep hot. Melt a tablespoonful or two of butter and when hot, throw in 6–12 boiled chestnuts broken in rough pieces. Add the sprouts, toss all together, season highly and serve.

Lightly fried onion rings and freshly chopped parsley are another delightful combination to add to cooked sprouts along with a walnut of butter. Or toss them in a little finely chopped raw onion and freshly chopped parsley.

Left-over cabbage and sprouts are nice fried with the breakfast bacon. *One oz. of chestnuts (with shells) contains* 10 *gm. of carbohydrate.*

LEEKS

Leeks are delicious, plain boiled, drained for ever, and served coated with melted butter or cream. They are good too, placed in a well-buttered casserole, covered with buttered paper, a tight-fitting lid, and baked in the oven or over a low heat. They can be smothered in grated cheese (after cooking) and glazed under the grill. Once when hard up for lettuce, I served a salad of cold cooked leeks, coated in French dressing, to partner some spring-run cold salmon. It was great. Try it. *Two small leeks contain* 5 *gm. of carbohydrate.*

BRAISED LEEKS

Fry a good-sized sliced onion until nicely brown. Drain free of fat and place in a casserole. Lay the prepared leeks on top, pour in some stock or good gravy to come half-way up the vegetables. Cover with a lid and cook in a moderate oven (about 350 deg.) for 45–60 minutes, or stand the dish on the grill-plate turned at low.

Leeks can be sandy, so split them through the centre to within ½ inch of the base, open them out and run the cold water through to free the grit. *Two small leeks contain 5 gm. of carbohydrate.*

SEAKALE

Wash and trim any coarse or discoloured pieces from the seakale. Tie in bundles and boil until tender in salted water, to which a good squeeze of lemon has been added. Time varies, for tough seakale can take an age. When tender, drain thoroughly and serve on toast coated with melted butter and freshly chopped parsley, or with cream seasoned with pepper, salt and a little tarragon vinegar. Not a favourite of ours. *Without toast this recipe contains negligible gm. of carbohydrate. One oz. of toast equals 15 gm. of carbohydrate.*

CURLY KALE

Pick only young tender leaves of kale and treat as you do cabbage or spinach. Old kale can be as tough as the pro-verbial old boots. Kale at its best is delicious, chock-a-block with vitamins and other good things. *Negligible carbohydrate.*

Vegetables

CHICORY (*Endive Belge*)

Not unlike seakale but more solid and can be prepared and cooked in the same way. *Negligible carbohydrate*.

ENDIVE

A plant with green curly leaves which is eaten raw as salad. Remove coarse discoloured outside leaves, trim off the stalk, wash well and put in cold salted water if necessary, to crisp. Drain and dry thoroughly, cut into quarters or eighths, and serve like lettuce, as a basis for salad or on its own dressed with French dressing (page 66), or mayonnaise (page 67). *Negligible carbohydrate*.

CELERIAC

The root of the turnip-rooted celery and just like a small round turnip in appearance with the same thick skin. Not a common vegetable but it has a nice flavour. Peel the celeriac, cut into small pieces and throw them into cold water as they discolour. Cook in boiling salted water until tender, 30 minutes or longer, drain thoroughly and serve with butter, freshly ground pepper and chopped parsley. Or they can be mashed, mixed with hot butter or cream and plenty of ground pepper. *Negligible carbohydrate*.

Vegetables

SWEDES

Peel and cut them in chunks. Boil in salted water until tender, 30 minutes or longer. Drain thoroughly, mash them and finish with a little hot butter and plenty of pepper. *Three tablespoons of swedes contain 5 gm. of carbohydrate.*

ASPARAGUS

To prepare asparagus, hold each stalk, towards the tip, in the left hand; gently scrape away the loose scales attached below the tip and scrape lightly to the end. Divide into small bundles with tips lying even and in the same direction. Tie bundles with clean string, cut stalks even at the bottom and leave in cold water until required.

When it is time to cook the prepared asparagus, put the bundles into boiling water with a pinch of sugar and plenty of salt. Boil gently (covered) until the green part below the tip is tender though firm—10–20 minutes. When tender remove carefully to a clean cloth and leave to drain thoroughly. Serve hot on a clean folded napkin without, of course, the string. Eat with melted butter. *Negligible carbohydrate.*

GLOBE ARTICHOKES

Cut away the stalks close to the bottom so that they stand evenly upright. Snip off the sharp pointed ends of the leaves and soak the heads for an hour in salted water, in which there is a trace of vinegar or lemon juice. Wash well under cold water, then cook in boiling salted water until a leaf will pull out easily, 30–60 minutes. Drain

thoroughly and serve on a folded napkin with a sauce-
boat of melted butter. *Negligible carbohydrate.*

BROAD BEANS

Broad beans should have the husks removed, either before
or after boiling. They are delicious finished off in a little
hot butter or cream, with a good pinch of chopped basil
added. Some freshly chopped mint is also good, as is
freshly chopped parsley. *Two level tablespoons of broad beans
contain* 10 *gm. of carbohydrate.*

SHRIMP, SWEETBREAD AND CELERY SALAD

Break up 2 cooked sweetbreads free of skin and gristle.
Mix with about twice their volume of potted or tinned
shrimps along with ¼ heart of celery diced. Mix all together in French dressing or mayonnaise. Serve as it is, or
surrounded with quarters of crisp lettuce heart and sprigs
of watercress. Celery, of course, is omitted when it is not
in season and diced chicken can replace the sweetbread.
This contains negligible carbohydrate.

RAW CARROT SALAD

*2 medium-sized raw carrots grated on the fine grater, a
suspicion of grated nutmeg, a piece of celery taken from
the heart and finely chopped, along with a morsel of finely
chopped raw onion and freshly chopped parsley.*

Mix all together and stir in some highly seasoned French
dressing.

Vegetables

If raw carrot is grated on the fine side of a grater after you have just grated nutmeg, the carrot has a lovely flavour. *One large carrot contains 5 gm. of carbohydrate.*

RAW SALADS

In the winter we eat raw salads almost daily. I usually serve them after the sweet course as a refresher. Most of the winter vegetables can be eaten raw, when finely grated or shredded. The best-known example is cabbage, which emerges as the classic cole slaw. It is time wasting to give set recipes for these salads. Small amounts of different vegetables can be used to give attractive combinations of colour and flavour. See that they are mixed with a highly seasoned dressing and, if some shredded leek isn't included, add a morsel of finely chopped raw onion and freshly chopped parsley.

Some minced or chopped salted peanuts as an occasional addition also lend charm. *These salads contain negligible carbohydrate.*

COLE SLAW

2 breakfastcupfuls of shredded raw cabbage, about a teaspoonful of finely chopped raw onion, 2 tablespoonfuls of chopped green pepper (optional), French dressing to mix and freshly chopped parsley for garnish.

Shred the cabbage from a tender heart and throw the shreds into cold water to crisp. When ready to serve, drain and dry the cabbage thoroughly. Mix with the other ingredients and add the dressing, tossing all together. Serve well chilled with the parsley sprinkled over. Good when lettuce is expensive and not at its best. The green pepper, when used, must have pips removed but need not be skinned. *Negligible carbohydrate.*

SALAD OF FRENCH OR RUNNER BEANS

Boil the sliced beans in well salted water until barely tender. Drain in a colander and at once let the cold water run over them to fix the colour. Let them drain thoroughly and get quite cold. When ready to serve, mix with them a suspicion of finely chopped raw onion or garlic (but the latter sparingly), add a generous supply of freshly chopped parsley or chervil, toss all together in a suitable dressing and serve well chilled.

Strips of boiled ham or cold fried bacon can be incorporated in the beans. *Negligible carbohydrate.*

NOTE. *When cooking vegetables to use in salad, run cold water over them as soon as they are cooked. This will keep them a nice colour.*

ORANGE AND WALNUT SALAD

2 large oranges, about 1 oz. walnuts roughly broken, quarters of lettuce heart, sprigs of watercress or some mustard and cress, freshly chopped parsley, French dressing.

Cut the oranges in segments, free of pith and membrane, and toss them in the dressing along with the parsley. Toss the walnuts in a little dressing too. When ready to serve mix them both together and pile in a pyramid with the lettuce and cress in alternate heaps surrounding. *One orange contains 10 gm. of carbohydrate.*

CELERY, APPLE AND RADISH

*Dice a dessert apple and some heart of celery. Mix with
3 or 4 crisp red radishes sliced, some finely chopped
parsley and, if liked, a morsel of raw onion chopped.*

Toss all together in French dressing and serve well
chilled. Diced cucumber can replace the celery. If no
radish is available use a rosy apple, washed, polished and
unpeeled. *One medium-sized apple contains 10 gm. of carbohydrate.*

SALAD DRESSINGS

FRENCH DRESSING

*2 tablespoonfuls olive oil, 1 dessertspoonful vinegar or
lemon juice, salt and plenty of freshly milled pepper.*

Put the pepper and salt in a basin, add the oil and stir in
the vinegar. Stir it well before using as the ingredients
part company when left standing. This can be made in
much larger quantities and stored in a well-corked bottle.
It will keep for ages. *Negligible carbohydrate.*

VINAIGRETTE SAUCE

Make French dressing as above but use double proportions. Add a tablespoonful each of chopped capers and
freshly chopped parsley along with some chopped chives
or very finely chopped shallot. This can be used as a

dressing or is good with calf's head or cold beef. *Negligible carbohydrate*.

QUICKLY MADE CREAM DRESSING

Mix some cream or milk-top with a little tarragon vinegar. Season to taste with salt and freshly ground pepper. *Negligible carbohydrate*.

HOLLANDAISE SAUCE

2 tablespoons wine vinegar, 2 tablespoons water, 2 yolks, 2 oz. margarine, pepper, salt and a dash of cayenne.

Put the vinegar on to boil with a shake of pepper or 2 peppercorns and let it boil until it is reduced to a table-spoonful. Remove the peppercorns, add the water (cold) and stir in the yolks. Stir over hot water until it begins to thicken then add the margarine a little at a time, whisking as you add. Finally season with salt and the cayenne. Hollandaise sauce is usually served warm as a sauce for poached fish or asparagus, but I have often let it get cold and used it as a salad dressing. *Negligible carbohydrate*.

MAYONNAISE

2 egg yolks, pinches of salt, pepper and dry mustard, about ½ pint olive oil and a little wine vinegar or lemon juice—about a tablespoonful.

Put the yolks and seasonings in a bowl and mix together. Gradually stir in the oil very slowly at first, or the eggs will curdle. As the sauce thickens add a drop or two of vinegar which will thin it a little, then back to the oil, adding it slowly and steadily (and thinning with vinegar when necessary) until the oil is used and the sauce is a nice thick consistency. Keep covered in a cold place.

Supposing your sauce curdles early on, then whisk in quickly a very little hot water. Or put a tablespoonful of boiling water in a basin and gradually beat in the curdled mixture. If that is unsuccessful then start all over again with one yolk and gradually add the curdled mixture after the first thinning down. *Negligible carbohydrate*.

TARTARE SAUCE

To ½ pint mayonnaise made as above, fold in carefully a tablespoonful each of chopped capers and chopped gherkins, a small shallot, very finely chopped, and a tablespoonful of freshly chopped parsley. *Negligible carbohydrate*.

Sweets

These are a selection of sweets that have been approved, out of the many experiments tried. Throughout, I refer to liquid sweetening as 'sweetex' and saccharine as 'saxin', not because of personal preference, but because they are easier words to write. Sometimes it is convenient to use one form of sweetening, sometimes another. Puddings where banana and bread are used are served only occasionally—as a change. The amount of sweetening given is but a guide, as personal taste varies so and too much artificial sweetening can be horrible.

LEMON PUDDING

2 teacups cold water, rind and juice of 1 large lemon, 4 or 5 Saxin, 2 tablespoonfuls (fairly level) cornflour, 2 eggs, yolks and whites separate.

Bring water, lemon juice and rind to the boil. Add the saxin and stir in the cornflour blended in a little cold water. Boil gently for 8 minutes, stirring continually. Meanwhile beat the egg-whites stiff and when the cornflour mixture is cooked pour it, a little at a time, into the whisked whites, whisking continually until all is added. Pour into a wetted mould and leave until quite cold. Turn out and serve with custard sauce made with the two yolks. *This recipe makes 2 servings. Each serving contains 10 gm. of carbohydrate.*

CUSTARD SAUCE

2 teacupfuls milk (small measure), lemon or orange rind or vanilla to flavour, 2 yolks, 2 Saxin.

Put the milk on to boil with the saxin and rind. Remove the flavouring, let the milk cool a little then mix it, a little at a time, into the beaten yolks. Return the mixture to the rinsed pan or to a double boiler, stir over a low heat until it thickens but do not let it boil. Remove from the heat but leave it in the pan until quite cold, whisking it occasionally to keep it smooth.

If your custard does curdle, or you see little knots forming, remove it from the heat and whisk like mad, when all should come well and smooth. *This recipe makes 4 servings. Each serving contains 5 gm. of carbohydrate.*

GINGER APPLE CREAM

¼ pint apple purée, ¼ pint milk, 2 Saxin, 1 teaspoonful custard powder, ¼ teaspoonful powdered ginger, 1 teaspoonful gelatine softened in 2 teaspoonfuls cold water, a squeeze of lemon juice, 1 tablespoonful of whipped cream, 1 small orange.

The apples should have been stewed with orange skin

Sweets

to flavour and saxin to sweeten, then rubbed through a strainer and measured.

Put milk and saxin on to boil. Thicken with the custard powder and ginger blended with a little milk. When boiling, add the gelatine and stir until the gelatine is dissolved and evenly mixed. Remove from the heat, stir in the apple *purée*, add the squeeze of lemon and leave to cool, stirring often. When cool but not set, stir in the whipped cream.

Cut the orange into neat segments free of pith and membrane and stir them into the cream as it begins to thicken. Pour into a wetted mould or glass, and leave to set. Serve with whipped cream or milk-top.

This makes a nice-sized pudding which he eats in one helping. *One serving contains 30 gm. of carbohydrate.*

RHUBARB PUDDING

4 oz. chopped rhubarb, 3 or 4 Saxin, about a tablespoonful water, ½ pint milk, 2 more Saxin, 1 egg, 2 oz. bread cubed (a slice about ½ inch thick) and grated nutmeg.

Put the rhubarb, 3 saxin and water in a pan and heat just long enough to melt the saxin. Pour into a well-buttered pie dish and scatter some grated nutmeg over.

Reserve a tablespoonful of milk and heat the rest with the 2 saxin, adding, if liked, lemon or orange to flavour. Separate the yolk and the white of the egg. Stir the tablespoonful of cold milk into the yolk and pour the hot milk gradually into it, whisking continually to prevent curdling. Cover the rhubarb with the cubed bread, pour the egg mixture over and leave to soak—about 20 minutes. Grate some nutmeg over and bake in a slow oven (about 325) for 30–40 minutes. Whip the white stiff, pile over the pudding and return to the oven until pale brown. Serve hot. Two servings. *Each serving contains 20 gm. of carbohydrate.*

GLORIFIED RHUBARB CUSTARD

> 8 *oz. rhubarb (about 6 thin sticks), 2 oz. chopped dates.*
> ¼ *teaspoonful powdered ginger, 4 Saxin dissolved in 2 tablespoonfuls of boiling water.*
>   Custard: ½ *pint milk, 2 Saxin, 2 eggs, a little vanilla and, if desired, a grating of nutmeg for the top.*

Wash the rhubarb and cut it in inch pieces. Tap the spoon containing the ginger gently over the rhubarb and mix all with the chopped dates. Place the mixture in a buttered pie dish and pour over the saxin dissolved in the boiling water.

Whisk the eggs, add the milk, two saxin and vanilla and pour it all over the fruit. Bake at 325 deg. until the custard is set. Ten minutes after you put the pudding in to bake, give all a stir up, grate the nutmeg over and return to the oven to finish cooking.

'This is a lovely pudding,' said he, the first time I did it. *This makes 2 servings. Each serving contains 25 gm. of carbohydrate.*

PRUNE FLUMMERY

> 5 *oz. prunes, 1 egg-white, Saxin if liked to sweeten, though the prunes are sweet in themselves.*

Soak the prunes overnight in water to more than cover. The following day stew them in the same water until tender, adding sweetening if desired. Pass through a sieve and when the *purée* is cold, fold in the stiffly beaten white. Enough for 2 fool-glasses. *Each serving contains 25 gm. of carbohydrate.*

ORANGE MERINGUE

1 oz. bread without crusts, 3 tablespoonfuls milk, 3 small fat oranges (rind and juice), 8 drops Sweetex, 1 oz. butter, 2 eggs.

Have the bread cut thin and lay it in a small deep greased oven dish, pour the milk over and leave to soak about 30 minutes. Grate the rind from all three oranges and mix with the juice, which should be a good ¾ teacupful. Cream the butter and mix it with the 2 yolks, add the orange juice and sweetex. Pour this over the bread and bake in a slow oven about 325 deg. for about 30 minutes. Whisk the whites stiff and pile them on the mixture then return to the oven for a further 10 minutes or so when the whites should be lightly brown. *This makes 2 servings. Each serving contains 20 gm. of carbohydrate.*

ORANGE SPONGE

Rind and juice of 2 fat oranges, juice of ½ lemon, about ½ pint of thin cream, 1 teaspoonful powdered gelatine, 1 dessertspoonful cold water, 6 drops Sweetex.

Soak the gelatine in the cold water. Add it to the grated orange rind and juice, bring to boil and leave to cool. Whip the cream and when it thickens a little add the sweetex, then the orange juice, etc., a little at a time, whisking continually. Finally add the lemon juice and whisk until all is thoroughly incorporated.

Pour into fool glasses and serve very cold. Lovely. I make this sweet with the milk-top from my milk, skimmed over 3 days and stored in the refrigerator. The orange juice should measure 1½ wineglasses. *This recipe makes 3 servings. Each serving contains 10 gm. of carbohydrate.*

APRICOT SOUFFLÉ

> 1 *teacupful of apricot purée made from stewed dried apricots, 1 egg, a rounded teaspoonful of powdered gelatine, a tablespoonful boiling water, a dash of finely grated lemon rind and a squeeze of lemon juice, 4 drops Sweetex (optional).*

Melt the gelatine in the hot water and separate the yolk and white of the egg. Beat the yolk over hot water until it becomes pale. Mix in the melted gelatine (strained if necessary) and continue whisking over the heat for a minute, then add the apricot pulp mixed with lemon rind and juice and remove from the heat. Add the sweetex if required. Beat for a few minutes. Whisk the egg-white until stiff, stir this into the *purée* and continue whisking until the mixture begins to thicken. Pour into a glass dish and leave to set. Decorate with blobs of cream and serve cold. This should set to a nice light consistency. When only one egg-white is being whisked, it is best done on a flat plate as it gives more. *This makes 2 servings. Each serving contains 15 gm. of carbohydrate.*

Sweets

MRS. HENLEY'S COFFEE SOUFFLÉ
(or fish soufflé)

1 carton natural yoghurt (5½ fl. oz.), 3 tablespoonfuls of strong black coffee, 3 leaves of gelatine softened in cold water and dissolved in hot, a few drops of sweetening (optional), a dessertspoonful of brandy, 3 whipped egg whites.

Mix the yoghurt, coffee and brandy together. Mix in the dissolved gelatine (about a rounded teaspoonful of powdered gelatine dissolved would be equal to the above amount of leaf gelatine). Taste it before you add the sweetening – it will always have a sharp flavour and I prefer it without sweetening. Finally fold in the egg white stiffly beaten. Pour into a soufflé dish which should have a supporting oiled band of grease-proof paper round it, for the mixture should come much above the rim of the soufflé dish. Leave to set. This is much improved by eating it with a dash of Tia Maria liqueur. Enough for 2 or 3 servings. *One serving contains 5 gm. of carbohydrate.*

A delicious savoury soufflé can be made with the same basic ingredients. Omit the coffee and flavouring, substitute instead flaked fish such as sardines, kipper (skinned and boned of course), lobster or crab.

CREAM CHEESE AND FRESH FRUIT

This is a simple variation of the classic Coeur à la Creme. To make it, fork up some mild cream cheese (Chambourcy is suitable) or cottage cheese. Add a little cream to soften it if required and serve it with raspberries or strawberries

75

or with the raspberries squashed through a sieve to make a purée. *Three oz. of raspberries or strawberries contain 5 gm. of carbohydrate.*

BLACKCURRANT FOOL

1 breakfastcupful of blackcurrant purée, the same amount of whipped cream, Sweetex to taste, a squeeze of lemon if available.

Mix the ingredients together and serve in a glass dish or in fool glasses.

To get this amount you will need about ¾ of a 2 lb. jar of home-bottled blackcurrants. Stew them with sweetening to taste so that they are easy to sieve. A squeeze of lemon is invaluable for bringing out the flavour of fruit, particularly strawberries. When bottling blackcurrants, intersperse a few young blackcurrant leaves with the berries (about 3 to a 2 lb. jar) and the flavour will be much improved. *Negligible carbohydrate.*

BLACKCURRANT MOUSSE

A 2-lb. jar of bottled blackcurrants or 1 lb. fresh, 4 or 5 Saxin, 1 egg, 5 tablespoonfuls thin cream or milk-top, 1 gill water, ¼ oz. gelatine plus 1 level teaspoonful gelatine, a squeeze of lemon, Sweetex as needed.

Empty the fruit into a saucepan, adding more water if there doesn't seem much, as you will need a ¼ pint juice. Add the saxin and stew gently until the skins are soft.

Strain them from their juice, measure the juice which

should be ¼ pint and into it stir the level teaspoonful gelatine dissolved in a tablespoonful hot water. Pour into a glass serving dish and leave to set. Now rub the currants through the sieve and you should get about a gill of thick smooth pulp.

Separate the yolk and white of the egg, mix the milk-top into the yolk, add sweetex or more saxin to taste and stand the basin over boiling water until the custard thickens, stirring often. When it gets too hot for your finger, remove it from the heat and leave to cool in the basin, stirring often. Put the ¼ oz. gelatine and the gill water on to warm and when boiling stir in the *purée* so that the gelatine gets evenly distributed. Turn it into a basin and leave to cool. When the *purée* shows signs of setting, whisk in the custard, add the squeeze of lemon and adjust sweetening. Finally whisk in the stiffly beaten egg-white. Pour into the glass dish on top of the jelly and leave to set. Decorate with rosettes of whipped cream if desired.

This is a lovely sweet particularly in the dead of winter. It certainly involves a little extra work but worth it for anybody on a restricted diet. 1 gill whipped cream can be substituted for the milk-top-egg-yolk custard but the whipped white must be added. Three to four servings. *Negligible carbohydrate.*

GRAPENUT ICE I

1 *oz. grapenuts,* 7 *oz. milk,* 1 *small tin evaporated milk.*

Soak the grapenuts in the milk for about an hour. Whisk the evaporated milk until thick, add the milk and nuts and pour into the freezing-tray. Freeze for about 2 hours but

Sweets

half-way through remove the mixture to a bowl, whisk it up to get it smooth, then return it to the tray to finish freezing. I like this ice without sweetening; he prefers it with a few drops Sweetex added, so please yourselves. *This makes 2 servings. Each serving contains 25 gm. of carbohydrate.*

GRAPENUT ICE II

7 oz. milk-top, 2 Saxin, 2 small eggs (separated), 1 oz. grapenuts, 1 small tin evaporated milk.

Make a custard sauce (page 70) with the milk-top, saxin and beaten yolks. Leave to cool in the pan and when quite cold add the grapenuts. Leave to soak for an hour. Finally whisk the evaporated milk until thick and the egg-whites stiff. Stir the milk into the grapenut mixture and fold in the whites. Pour into the freezing-tray and freeze for about 2 hours giving it a whisk up half-way through. Four servings.

Both these ices are delicious.

For those who are chary of grapenuts, bran might be substituted, but I have never tried it, so cannot advise. *This makes 4 servings. Each serving contains 10 gm. of carbohydrate.*

BANANA ICE

2 small bananas, 2 large eggs, ½ pint milk, 2 Saxins, a spot of vanilla essence, and a squeeze of lemon, 4 drops Sweetex.

Separate the yolks and whites of the eggs. Make a custard sauce with the yolks, milk and saxin as described on page 70.

When the custard is quite cold, mash the bananas with a fork and add them to the custard along with the vanilla, sweetex and lemon juice. Finally fold in the stiffly beaten whites, pour into the freezing-tray and freeze about 2 hours. A lovely sweet, as it tastes of banana. No doubt a spoonful of whipped cream added would make it heaven sent, but it is delicious without. *This makes 2 servings. Each serving contains* 15 *gm. of carbohydrate.*

MELON ICE CREAM

1 ripe Ogen melon, 2 eggs separated, a teacupful of milk, ½ pt. double cream, a few drops of sweetening and Kirsch to flavour.

Make a custard sauce with the beaten yolks and milk and sweeten to taste. Leave to cool stirring occasionally. It should be fairly thick.

Peel and seed the melon and cut it into neat dice. Whip the cream not too stiffly and mix into it the cold custard sauce along with the melon. Flavour with a teaspoonful or two of Kirsch, taste for sweetening, add a squeeze of lemon, pour into the freezing tray and partially freeze.

Whip up the egg white stiffly. Remove the melon cream into a bowl and beat smooth. Stir in the whipped whites, return to the freezing tray and freeze to a smooth consistency. *One oz. of melon contains* 10 *gm. of carbohydrate and* 1 *teacupful of milk* 10 *gm.*

Sweets

BANANA CREAM I

2 bananas, 7 tablespoonfuls of thin cream or milk-top, 2 Saxin or Sweetex to taste, a teaspoonful of rum, a grating of nutmeg for the top, 1 yolk.

Butter a deep dish and in it lay the bananas peeled and cut in half. Whip the cream until frothy, add the rum, sweetening and yolk then pour the mixture over the bananas. Grate the nutmeg over the top and bake at 350 deg. until very lightly set—about 30 minutes. A delicious sweet—smooth and velvety. *This makes 2 servings. Each serving contains 10 gm. of carbohydrate.*

STEAMED COCONUT PUDDING

1 rounded teaspoonful of flour, 1 egg (separated), 4 tablespoonfuls milk, 1 tablespoonful desiccated coconut, a grating of lemon rind and 5 drops Sweetex.

Mix the egg-yolk with the flour. Add the milk slowly to avoid lumps. Add the coconut, lemon rind and sweetex. Whisk the egg-white stiff and add to it the egg-yolk mixture by degrees, whisking the white continually as you add. Pour the mixture into a small greased pudding basin, cover with buttered paper and steam gently for about 30 minutes. Turn out and serve at once. This is a nice sweet and tastes of coconut. My husband liked it. It makes a nice-sized sweet but hardly enough for two. *The one serving contains 10 gm. of carbohydrate.*

Sweets

STEAMED CHOCOLATE PUDDING

1 rounded teaspoonful each self-raising flour and cocoa, 1 egg (separated), 4 tablespoonfuls milk, about 5 drops Sweetex and a little vanilla.

Mix the flour and cocoa together. Add the yolk and a little of the milk and blend to a smooth paste. Add the rest of the milk gradually to avoid lumps. Whisk the egg-white stiff and add to it the cocoa mixture whisking the white continually as you add. Flavour with a little vanilla, add the sweetex and pour into a greased small pudding bowl. Cover with buttered paper and steam gently for about 30 minutes. *This makes one serving which contains 10 gm. of carbohydrate.*

HOT APRICOT SOUFFLÉ

1 large egg (separated), ¼ pint milk, a scrap of lemon rind, 1 Saxin, a good-sized dessertspoonful of diabetic apricot jam.

Make a custard sauce as described on page 70, with the yolk, milk, lemon rind and saxin. Leave to cool.

For the *soufflé*, whisk the white stiff. Add the jam and continue whisking for a moment or two then turn it into a small greased pudding basin. Cover with greased paper and steam gently for about 15 minutes when it should be set. Turn on to a hot plate and cover with the custard sauce. D. loves this sweet as the lemon-flavoured sauce contrasts well with the apricot. *This one serving contains 5 gm. of carbohydrate.*

81

Sweets

VELVET CREAM

*½ pint thin cream, 1 teaspoonful gelatine, juice of ½
lemon, 1 tablespoonful water, 1 wineglass of dry white
wine, 6 drops Sweetex.*

Soak the gelatine in the lemon juice and leave it for a
time, it will swell a little and become powdery. Add the
water to it and stir it over the heat until it becomes hot
liquid. Strain it into a cup.

Whisk the cream until it becomes frothy. Gradually add
the gelatine while it is still warm and continue whisking.
Now add the wine, instalment fashion, whisking all the
time. Lastly add the sweetex and whisk until the cream
leaves a trail. Pour into individual glasses and leave to set.
Two greedy servings.

His favourite sweet. It's a lovely sweet with a delicate
flavour; and once you have the gelatine melted and the
whisking begins, it should take no more than 15 minutes
until it is ready to set. As for the orange sponge, I use
milk-top salvaged from 3 days' milk and stored in the
refrigerator. *Negligible carbohydrate.*

EGG JUNKET

*1 pint milk, 1 beaten egg, 1 teaspoonful vanilla essence,
3 or 4 drops Sweetex, 1 teaspoonful rennet, nutmeg.*

Beat the egg thoroughly, mix in the milk. Stir over a
gentle heat until it is too hot to bear your finger in, so
that the egg cooks a little. Add vanilla and sweetex and
pour into a glass dish. When it cools to blood heat, stir in

the rennet and leave to set. Serve icy cold with a scatter of grated nutmeg on top. Good, especially with stewed rhubarb. *This recipe makes 3 servings. Each serving contains 10 gm. of carbohydrate.*

ORANGE CREAM

2 eggs, juice of 2 fat oranges, finely grated rind of one, squeeze of lemon, 3 drops of Sweetex.

Separate yolk and white of one of the eggs. Put the yolk and whole egg together in a small basin and beat well. Whisk in the orange juice (there should be 3 liquid ounces) and add the orange rind and lemon juice. Stand the basin over a pan of cold water and let it come to boil. Stir the orange mixture from time to time and when it gets thick remove it from the heat. Leave to cool, stirring occasionally. Stir in the sweetex and when cold fold in the stiffly beaten white of egg. Turn into 2 individual glasses. This would make a nice spread for tea. *Each serving contains 10 gm. of carbohydrate.*

RHUBARB MOUSSE

½ pint sieved stewed rhubarb, 6 tablespoonfuls cream (or undiluted evaporated milk), ¼ oz. gelatine dissolved in 2 tablespoonfuls rhubarb juice, a squeeze of lemon and Sweetex to taste.

Soak the gelatine in the measured juice and melt it over a low heat. Add the *purée* to it and stir until all is warm so that the gelatine is evenly distributed. Leave to cool.

Whisk the cream until thick, combine it with the *purée*, add the lemon juice and sweetex, and stir occasionally until nearly setting. Pour into a glass dish and serve cold. *This makes 2 servings. Each serving contains negligible carbohydrate, but if evaporated milk is used. 5 gm.*

CARRAGHEEN

½ oz. carragheen, 1 pint milk, a piece of lemon rind, 3-inch piece of cinnamon, 3 or 4 Saxin and a pinch of salt.

Wash the carragheen. Put it in the milk along with the flavouring, saxin and a pinch of salt. Bring to boil and simmer gently for 8 minutes. Remove the rind and cinnamon, run the milk through a strainer and leave it until quite cold when it will set like blancmange.

Carragheen is a seaweed, found in the Outer Hebrides and Ireland. It can be purchased in packet form but isn't as good as that grown in our own islands. *This makes 3 servings. Each serving contains 10 gm. of carbohydrate.*

HOT FRUIT SALAD

2 Cox's orange pippins, 1 large orange, 1 banana, 1 oz. butter, a small level teaspoonful powdered cinnamon, 4 drops Sweetex, a squeeze of lemon.

Peel and core the apples and cut into wedges. Peel the bananas, cutting them in two, if necessary, and cut the peeled orange crosswise in thick slices. Lay all in a buttered shallow fire-proof dish. Squeeze the lemon over. Make a paste of the butter, cinnamon and sweetex, adding too a squeeze of lemon. Put blobs of it over the fruit.

Bake in a moderately hot oven for about 20 minutes and serve hot. If you don't want to put the oven on, turn the grill-plate to 'low', when it is warm stand the dish on it. Leave it for about 20 minutes, basting the fruit with the melted butter towards the end. Finally switch the grill to 'high' and stand the dish under until the fruit is glazed— about 5 minutes. A pleasing sweet. *This makes 4 servings. Each serving contains 10 gm. of carbohydrate.*

FRUIT JUNKET

> 1 *dessert apple peeled and cut in wedges*, 1 *banana peeled and sliced, a grating of nutmeg and some whipped cream or milk top.* 1 *pint milk*, 1 *teaspoonful rennet.*

Lay the mixed fruit in a glass dish. Warm the milk to blood heat, stir in the rennet and pour it over the fruit. When quite cold and firm, grate the nutmeg over and cover with whipped cream.

This was something I first tried one Whit Monday and it proved a great success, the flavour of the fruit, nutmeg and cream blending together in a most pleasing friendship. The evening before I set 2 pints of milk in a basin, skimmed it for the whipped cream on the following day, and made the junket with what was left. Two servings. *Each serving contains 25 gm. of carbohydrate.*

BAKED CUSTARD

> 3 *eggs*, 1 *pint milk*, 4 *Saxin*, 1 *teaspoonful vanilla, grated nutmeg.*

Warm the milk to dissolve the saxin. Stir it into the beaten eggs and vanilla flavouring. Strain into a greased pie dish, scatter the grated nutmeg on top and bake at

300 deg. F. for about 40 minutes.

This may look a little soft in the middle when you remove it from the oven, but the heat in the pie dish should be enough to finish it. This gives a custard of a light, smooth consistency. Or heat an electric oven to 450 deg., put in the custard and switch off at once. Bake 20–30 minutes. *This makes 3 servings. Each serving contains 10 gm. of carbohydrate.*

ROLLED OATS CUSTARD

½ oz. rolled oats, 1 pint milk, 4 Saxin, 2 or 3 eggs, a teaspoonful vanilla, grated nutmeg.

Put the oats in the oven or under the grill just to toast them slightly. Make the custard as above, stir in the oats and bake as above. Give the oats a stir up once or twice during the early part of the cooking. Two servings. *Each serving contains 20 gm. of carbohydrate.*

COCONUT CUSTARD

2 eggs, ½ pint milk, 3–4 Saxin, thin pieces of lemon rind, 2 rounded tablespoonfuls coconut, grated nutmeg on top.

Put milk, saxin and lemon rind on to get really hot so that the lemon flavour is extracted. Let it cool before mixing it into the beaten eggs. Strain into a greased pie dish, mix in the coconut, scatter the nutmeg over and bake as for baked custard. *This makes 1 serving which contains 15 gm. of carbohydrate.*

Sweets

BREADCRUMB PUDDING

*¾ pint milk, 4 Saxin, thin lemon rind, 1 oz. fine bread-
crumbs, walnut of butter, 2 eggs, a grating of nutmeg.*

Bring milk to boil with lemon rind and saxin. Strain it
over the crumbs and butter and leave until fairly cool,
about 15 minutes. Whisk in by degrees the beaten eggs
and turn it into a greased pie dish. Bake at 300 deg. until
lightly set (30–40 minutes). After the first 10 minutes'
cooking, remove the pudding from the oven, give it a
stir up to distribute the crumbs, grate the nutmeg over
the surface and return it to the oven to finish cooking.
Good hot or cold. Two servings. *Each serving contains 20 gm.
of carbohydrate.*

NEEDWOOD GOOSEBERRIES

*1 lb. unripe gooseberries topped and tailed (or use 1 pint of
bottled), 4 Saxin or more to sweeten, 1 oz. flour, 2 eggs,
1 teacupful milk, grated orange rind, 2 tablespoonfuls
melted margarine.*

If the gooseberries are bottled, make them hot enough to
melt the saxin, then you can taste them for sweetening. If
using fresh fruit, stew them a little first with of course the
sweetening.

Separate the yolks and whites of the eggs. Mix the
flour, yolks and a little of the milk to a smooth paste, then
gradually add the rest of the milk, taking care to keep the
batter lump-free. Add grated orange rind to flavour, the
melted margarine and sweetex to taste. Lastly fold in the

stiffly beaten egg-whites. Pour this mixture over the fruit and bake in a moderate oven (350 deg. F.) for about 40 minutes, when it should have a nice golden crust. Serve warm, rather than hot. This should make three generous servings. *Each serving contains 10 gm. of carbohydrate.*

APPLE FLOAT

2 eggs, ½ pint milk, 2 Saxin, flavouring such as lemon rind, vanilla or about ½ teaspoonful of orange flower water, 1 Cox's orange pippin or russet apple, about 4 drops Sweetex.

Separate yolks and whites of the eggs. Make a custard sauce with the yolks, milk, saxin and flavouring as directed under Lemon Pudding (page 69). When the custard is quite cold pour it into a shallow glass dish for serving.

About an hour before serving time, peel, core and grate the apple. Whisk the egg-whites stiff. Add the apple in two or three lots and continue whisking until quite stiff. Finally add the sweetex and whisk again so that it is evenly distributed. Pile it in blobs over the custard. Serve icy cold.

A really lovely sweet and when I used orange flower water to flavour the custard he thought it was a nice liqueur. *This makes 2 servings. Each serving contains 10 gm. of carbohydrate.*

Sweets

BANANA CREAM II

5 bananas, small tin evaporated milk (undiluted) or an equivalent amount of cream, 1 oz. diabetic chocolate, 1 oz. shelled walnuts, ½ oz. gelatine, ½ gill water, 1 egg-white beaten stiff.

Grate the chocolate, chop the walnuts and mash the bananas—they should make ½ pint pulp. Whisk the milk or cream, stir in the chocolate, walnuts and pulp. Sweeten to taste, but we leave ours without. Make the gelatine and water quite hot in a saucepan and strain it into the mixture. Mix quickly and thoroughly and leave for a few minutes, stirring occasionally. When it begins to thicken, fold in the stiffly beaten egg-white and turn into a rinsed mould or glass dish. Serve cold, four good servings. A sweet to have only on State occasions and not at all if you're a Conformist. *If evaporated milk is used, each serving contains 15 gm. of carbohydrate, without evaporated milk 10 gm.*

CHOCOLATE MOUSSE

A cake (3 oz.) diabetic chocolate, 2 tablespoonfuls cold water, about 8 drops olive oil, a few drops vanilla essence, 2 eggs (separated).

Break the chocolate into a large basin, add the water and oil. Stand it over a pan of boiling water until the chocolate is melted. Remove the basin from the heat and mix the chocolate evenly smooth. Mix in the yolks, one at a time, add the vanilla and finally the stiffly beaten egg-whites. Turn into a glass dish and leave until quite set. Best made a day in advance.

Sweets

A few drops of strong coffee can be added if desired or a pinch of powdered cinnamon can be put with the chocolate, as it brings out the flavour. Two servings. *Negligible carbohydrate.*

CHOCOLATE WALNUT MOUSSE

1 teacupful plus a tablespoonful milk, 1 heaped teaspoonful of cocoa, a level teaspoonful gelatine, 2 Saxin or 4 drops Sweetex, a few drops of vanilla, 2 tablespoonfuls chopped walnuts (about 1 oz.).

Blend the cocoa with a little of the milk and put it in a saucepan with the rest of the milk and the gelatine. Stir until boiling and boil for about a minute to cook the cocoa. If saxin is being used add it now too. Pour it into a basin and leave to get quite cold. Whisk it up and when it begins to thicken add the vanilla, walnuts and sweetex to taste. Turn into a rinsed mould or glass dish. Serve cold with cream or milk-top. Makes a lightly set mousse, just enough for one. *One serving contains 15 gm. of carbohydrate.*

CHOCOLATE CREAM BERGÉ

2 oz. butter, 2 eggs (separated,) 2 oz. melted diabetic chocolate, ½ teaspoonful each brandy and rum.

Cream the butter. Add the 2 yolks by degrees, then the chocolate (which can be melted in a basin over boiling water), then the flavouring and finally mix in the whites, stiffly beaten. Turn into a glass serving dish and leave in the coldest place for 24 hours. A lovely rich sweet. *This contains negligible carbohydrate.*

BAKED APPLES

2 cooking apples, ½ oz. butter, 8 drops Sweetex, ¼ level teaspoonful powdered cinnamon, ginger or ground cloves, about a tablespoonful water.

Make a paste with the butter, sweetex and flavouring. Wash the apples and core them. Fill each cavity with the paste, slit the peel a little to prevent bursting and, if liked, stab with a clove or two. Place in a buttered baking dish, add the water, cover with buttered paper and bake in a moderate oven 20–30 minutes, basting them occasionally during the cooking. These are best, I think, with ginger.

When the apple crop is harvested, he loves one or two baked apples at night. Rather than put the oven on, I place the prepared apples, in a small deep buttered Pyrex dish with a lid, then stand it on the grill-plate which has been previously heated by switching on to 'low'. They cook nice-and-quietly within the hour. *This makes 2 servings. Each serving contains 15 gm. of carbohydrate.*

APPLE PANCAKE

4 oz. flour sifted with a pinch of salt, 1 egg, milk and warm water to mix to a thin cream. 1 dessertspoonful orange flower water, liquid sweetening to taste, 1 Cox's orange pippin peeled, cored and cut in slices, a little hot lard for frying (or use butter), cream to accompany.

Drop the egg, whole, into the flour, add a little of the liquid and mix smooth. Continue adding the liquid until you get a lump-free batter of the consistency of thin cream. Add flavouring and sweetening and leave for an hour.

When ready to serve, heat a small frying-pan (about 7 inches) on top of the grill. Melt a nugget of butter or lard therein and when it is smoking hot swill it round the sides. Pour in enough batter to cover thinly the bottom, leave to cook for a moment, then on it dispose some of the apple. Again leave for a minute or two until you think the bottom is cooked. Now spoon over a little more batter, just enough to cover the apples and stand the pan under the grill but resting only on the oven top. Leave to cook for a further few minutes until the top is brown. Slide on to the hot serving dish and eat at once. Use the rest of the batter in the same way. Should make three hefty servings. *Each serving contains 30 gm. of carbohydrate.*

EVE'S PUDDING I.

4 *small apples peeled, cored and sliced, 3 or 4 saxin dissolved in about ½ teacupful of hot water, a walnut of margarine and some grated nutmeg. 1 oz. self-raising flour, ½ oz. soya flour, grated rind of ½ small orange, ½ oz. margarine, 2 tablespoonfuls orange juice, 1 egg, Sweetex to taste.*

Put the sliced apples in a well-buttered Pyrex dish along with the sweetened water and the walnut of margarine. Scatter the nutmeg on top.

Mix the flour, soya flour and orange rind. Rub in the ½ ounce of margarine and mix to a soft consistency with the beaten egg and orange juice. Add a few drops of sweetex to taste and pour the batter over the apples. Bake at 375 deg. for about 35 minutes. Serve hot with milk-top.

This pudding looks odd but we both enjoyed it—the orange and nutmeg flavour are a delightful combination. *This makes 2 servings. Each serving contains 20 gm. of carbohydrate.*

EVE'S PUDDING II.

3 medium-sized cooking apples, peeled, cored and sliced, 4 saxin dissolved in ½ teacupful water, a grating of nutmeg if liked, 1 rounded dessertspoonful self-raising flour, 1 oz. margarine, 2 eggs (separated), 4 dessertspoonfuls milk, Sweetex to taste, grating of lemon rind.

Put the apples in a buttered Pyrex dish with the sweetened water and sprinkle on nutmeg if it is to be used.

Put the flour in a basin, cut in the margarine and gradually work it to a smooth paste. Blend in the yolks a little at a time and then add the milk. At this stage the mixture curdles, but carry on. Grate in a little lemon rind, add sweetex to taste and finally fold in the whites stiffly beaten. Adjust sweetening if desired, pour the mixture over the apples and bake at 300 deg. for 45 minutes or longer. Serve hot for two. This fits into my natty 6-inch diameter deep Pyrex dish which holds one pint. A delicious sweet. *Each serving contains 20 gm. of carbohydrate.*

Sweets

POIRES AU CASSIS

2 medium-sized dessert pears, about 6 dessertspoonfuls blackcurrant purée.

Stew the blackcurrants with 2 or 3 saxin until soft enough to sieve. Squash through a nylon strainer. The *purée* should be of a coating consistency and fairly tart.

Half, peel and core the pears and lay them, round side up, in the serving dish. Coat with the *purée* and serve, well chilled, either as they are or with junket. A good way of using woolly pears. If you are working with hard pears, first stew them until tender. Drain them free of juice and put some of the juice with the blackcurrants while stewing. For those like D. who insist on a good helping of steak and kidney pudding, this is a good sweet to follow. *One medium-sized pear contains 15 gm. of carbohydrate.*

STEWED PEARS

1½ lb. pears, 2 or 3 pieces lemon rind, 4 Saxin, cold water barely to cover.

Peel the pears, cut in half and remove the core with a sharp-pointed knife. Put in a saucepan with the lemon rind, water and saxin, bring to boil and simmer until tender (1–1½ hours). These are delicious and taste very much like tinned pears. *Four oz. of stewed pears contain 10 gm. of carbohydrate.*

Sweets

COFFEE JELLY

½ pint freshly made strong black coffee (hot), 2 rounded teaspoonfuls gelatine dissolved in 2 tablespoonfuls boiling water, Saxin to taste or none at all if you don't take it in coffee, a teaspoonful brandy, rum, whisky or liqueur.

Make the coffee strong and strain it through fine muslin. Add the hot liquid gelatine, saxin and flavouring and strain into a rinsed mould to set. Serve with whipped cream. One serving. *This contains negligible carbohydrate.*

MILK JELLY

½ pint milk, 1 rounded teaspoonful gelatine, 2 Saxin, scraps of lemon or orange rind, or some vanilla essence.

Put the gelatine in the cold milk and let it soak for about 5 minutes. Add the saxin and flavouring and bring to boil, stirring all the time in case some of the gelatine sticks to the bottom. Strain into a basin and leave to cool. Stir occasionally until it begins to thicken, then pour it into a wetted mould to set. Serve with stewed fruit. *This 1 serving contains 15 gm. of carbohydrate.*

SUSSEX PUDDING

Have some stewed and sweetened blackcurrants in a glass dish. Make some milk jelly as above, using double portions and omitting the flavouring. When it begins to thicken, pour it over the fruit and leave to set. *Blackcurrants contain negligible carbohydrate.*

EGG JELLY

2 eggs, 1 lemon, juice and rind, cold water to make the lemon juice up to ½ pint, 1 rounded teaspoonful gelatine, Saxin or Sweetex to taste.

Grate the lemon on the fine grater, squeeze the juice and make it up to ½ pint with the water. Put the gelatine, lemon rind and a good half of the liquid in a pan and stir until boiling. Sweeten provisionally. Beat the eggs and mix in the rest of the cold liquid, then whisk in what you brought to boil. Return all to the rinsed pan, and stir over a gentle heat so that the egg cooks a little, but don't let it boil. Adjust sweetening, leave in the pan to cool a little, stirring occasionally, then pour into a wetted mould to set. Orange can replace the lemon but the flavour is more insipid and you would need to add a good squeeze of lemon to ginger things up. *Negligible carbohydrate.*

POMMES ROUSSEL

Put some well-flavoured apple *purée* in a glass dish or in fool glasses. Grate some diabetic chocolate over and cover with whipped cream. *Five oz. contain 10 gm. of carbohydrate.*

Sweet

HONEYCOMB CREAM

1 pint milk, 2 rounded teaspoonfuls gelatine, 4 Saxin, piece of lemon rind, 2 eggs separated, a good squeeze of lemon juice.

Soak the gelatine in the milk for about 5 minutes, then put the milk on to boil with the lemon rind and saxin. Stir to prevent the gelatine sticking to the bottom. Beat the yolks and add the strained milk a little at a time at first. Return the mixture to the pan and stir until boiling (yes, boiling!) Remove the pan from the heat, whisk the whites stiff and stir them into the egg. Add the lemon juice and pour into a wetted mould to set.

The final result should have a jelly top and creamy base, with the texture light, so don't be too generous with gelatine. Three to four servings. *One of 3 servings contains 10 gm. of carbohydrate.*

LEMON CURD

2 lemons, 2 oz. butter, Saxin to taste (about 6), 2 eggs and a few drops of Sweetex if desired.

Grate the lemons and squeeze out the juice. Put the butter, with lemon juice and rind, in a pan to melt. Add the saxin and when all is liquid mix it into the well beaten eggs. Stand the basin over boiling water and let it cook until it gets thick, stirring occasionally. Taste for sweetening and add a few drops sweetex if desired. When cool turn into a small tumbler. Nice instead of jam, or as a filling for tartlets. *This contains negligible carbohydrate.*

Sweet

WATER ICES

Water ices are easily made. Most fruit can be squashed through a fine sieve or liquidized to give either a purée or liquid which, when frozen to a soft consistency, makes a refreshing sweet course.

PINEAPPLE WATER ICE

Slice and skin the pineapple. Cut into sections and remove the hard core. Put the sections through a Mouli grater or liquidizer. The result will be a liquid not a purée. Flavour it with a teaspoonful or so of Kirsch, add a squeeze of lemon, pour into a bowl or freezing tray and freeze to a soft consistency stirring it occasionally to keep it from going rocky. A delicious refreshing ice. *Three oz. of pineapple juice contain* 10 *gm. of carbohydrate.*

RASPBERRY WATER ICE

Squash some fresh raspberries, through a fine sieve. Flavour the purée with a little Kirsch, mix in a squeeze of lemon juice and freeze. Strawberries and loganberries can also be treated in the same way, as can frozen raspberries. *Six oz. of raspberries or strawberries contain* 10 *gm. of carbohydrate.*

Pastries

Like most heavy smokers, my husband never seems to crave for sweets or cake and seldom eats any except when he has a reaction. What he is very fond of is home-made yeast mixtures made with ordinary flour and plate pies, such as apple, which can be served hot for pudding and cold for tea.

APPLE PLATE PIE

Short pastry made from 4 oz. flour, 1 medium-sized cooking apple, peeled, cored and cut in wedges, 12 drops Sweetex mixed in a dessertspoonful cold water, powdered cinnamon, grated nutmeg or ground cloves to flavour and ½ oz. margarine.

Divide the pastry into two and line a greased 8-inch shallow dish with one half rolled wafer thin. Lay the apple over, sprinkle the sweetex and flavouring on top and dot with the margarine. Wet the edges and cover with rest of the pastry very thinly rolled. Pinch the edges firm,

brush over, if liked, with milk or egg and milk and bake
at 375 for about 35 minutes. Pierce the pastry here and
there when you remove it from the oven. *This can make 8
small servings, each serving containing* 10 *gm. of carbohydrate.*

CITRON APPLE PASTRY

Quantities for paste and apple as above, but chop the
apple and mix it with a square inch each of citron and
orange peel and omit the spices. Scrape the peel free of
sugar and wash in warm water before using. D. says this
pie has a special flavour—it must be the citron. *See above
recipe for carbohydrate value.*

LEMON PIE

*About 2 oz. short pastry thinly rolled. 1 oz. flour, 2
tablespoonfuls margarine, 10–12 drops Sweetex, 2 eggs
(separated), rind and juice of 1 lemon, a teacupful milk.*

Soften the margarine and sweetex together and when
quite soft, add the yolks, flour, rind and juice of lemon
and milk. Finally fold in the stiffly beaten egg-whites.
Line an 8-inch shallow dish with pastry rolled paper thin,
pour in the mixture and bake at 350 deg. for about 40
minutes, or until golden brown. This makes a lovely cake
for tea. Once when I made it I forgot the milk and pastry.
It turned out rather like a Madeira cake. *This makes 4
servings. Each serving contains* 15 *gm. of carbohydrate.*

Pastries

CUSTARD TART

*A scrap of short pastry (about 2 oz.) very thinly rolled,
2 eggs, ½ pint milk, pieces of lemon rind, 4 Saxin,
grated nutmeg.*

Line a greased shallow Pyrex dish with the pastry thinly
rolled and prick it all over. Put milk, lemon rind and
saxin on to boil. Leave to cool and gradually mix it into
the beaten eggs. Strain into the pastry, grate nutmeg over
and bake at 400 deg. for about 36 minutes, or until the
custard is lightly set. If the custard has risen, prick it
lightly and it should flatten. Nice hot or cold. *This makes 4
servings. Each serving contains 10 gm. of carbohydrate.*

LEMON OR ORANGE CURD TARTLETS

Scraps of pastry can be thinly rolled to fit greased patty
tins. Prick them inside and bake, pricking them half-way
through the baking if they blister. When cooked fill them
with lemon curd (page 97), or orange cream (page 83).
Scatter chopped nuts on top and serve for tea. *One oz. of
cooked pastry contains 15 gm. of carbohydrate.*

MY OWN WHITE BREAD

To me, yeast mixtures are not half as troublesome to
make as scone mixtures. Maybe because my rolls and
bread are invariably more successful than my scones or
pancakes. Certainly yeast baking needs more time, but

you can do quite a lot, or have a rest, in between, starting and finishing.

> 1 *lb. plain flour sieved with a teaspoonful salt,* 1 *oz. butter or pure lard,* ½ *oz. yeast, about* ½ *pint tepid milk and water.*

Put the flour in a basin. Rub in the butter. Make a well in the centre, crumble in yeast and pour in milk and water gradually. Mix until you get a fairly moist dough. Leave it in the basin and put it to rise, covered with a cloth, in a warm draught-free corner. I choose a linen cupboard where the hot tank is. It will need about an hour or longer, because it should rise to double its bulk. When risen turn it on to a floured board, dust lightly with flour and knead lightly sides to middle, 6 or 8 times. Cut in half and put one half in a small loaf tin greased with butter or dripping or lard. Shape the other into a torpedo-shaped roll, or into 6 dinner rolls, and lay on a floured tin. Put to rise again for about 20 minutes, in the space between the cooking plates and oven or on top of a warm stove. Score the roll with a sharp knife in two places. Then put it and the loaf in the oven at 450 deg. Bake at that temperature for 20 minutes, then reduce the heat to 400 deg. F. The roll cooks in 30 minutes, the small rolls in 20 minutes and the tin about 45 minutes. When you remove them from the oven have some melted butter handy and brush them over with it, then cool on a wire tray. If I've had the yeast (compressed) in hand for a day or two and it looks a little dry, I sometimes sprinkle a teaspoonful of sugar over the yeast after crumbling it into the flour.

So when I want a new loaf on my tea table, which is quite often, I start mixing the flour about 2 p.m. Once it's in the linen cupboard I forget it and go out with the dogs, or hop on my bike down to our nice village shop-cum-post-office, two miles away. Have a few quiet minutes in our nice church while there, and by the time I'm back home my dough is ready for kneading and the second rising (proving). The bread tin I use is the size and shape of a small Hovis. *One oz. of bread contains 15 gm. of carbohydrate.*

GRANARY LOAF

> 1 *lb. granary breadmix flour*, 1 *teaspoonful salt*, ½ *oz. compressed yeast*, 1 *teaspoonful brown sugar*, 3 *oz. stoned raisins, a good ½ pint tepid milk and water.*

Mix the flour and salt in a basin. Add the stoned raisins. Cream the yeast and sugar, pour into it most of the tepid liquid and leave for about 5 minutes, when the yeast should froth to the surface. Stir this into the flour and mix all to a fairly soft dough, adding the rest of the liquid if necessary. Cover with a cloth and put to rise in a draught-free corner for about an hour when it should be double in bulk. Turn on to a floured board, knead lightly sides to middle 6 or 8 times, cut in two and shape into small round loaves. Place on greased and floured tins and put to rise between oven and cooking plates for about 25 minutes. Bake at 450 deg. F. for the first 15 minutes and switch to 400 deg. F. for the last 15 minutes, making 30 minutes in all. Brush with melted butter when you take them from the oven and cool on a wire tray. These are delicious loaves. Granary breadmix flour is made by the English Grains Company, Burton-on-Trent. *One oz. contains 15 gm. of carbohydrate.*

Pastries

CROISSANTS

(Mrs. B. Gould Marks)

½ lb. plain flour sifted with ½ teaspoonful salt, ½ ounce compressed yeast, ¼ pint tepid milk and water, 4 oz. butter.

Put the sifted flour and salt in a basin. Make a well in the centre, crumble in the yeast and pour in nearly all the liquid. Mix to a fairly soft dough, adding the rest of the liquid as desired. Cover and leave to rise for about 1 hour until double its size.

Now turn it on to a floured board, roll it into a strip and cover with the butter cut in small pieces. Dust it very lightly with flour and fold the strip in three, as with puff pastry. Press the edges together with the rolling-pin and indent also in the centre then give a half-turn. Roll out a second time, sprinkle lightly with flour then fold and turn as before. Cover with a cloth wrung out in cold water and leave for several hours, or overnight, in a cold place.

The next step is to roll and fold as described, making three in all. Then roll out for the fourth and final time into an oblong about ⅛ inch thick. Cut in half length-ways and put the two pieces on top of each other. Cut the double strip into equilateral triangles with 5-inch sides.

Separate the triangles. Take one at a time, hold the apex in the left hand while you roll up the base with the palm of the right hand like a cigar. Place these on the baking sheet with the points upwards and bend into a horseshoe. Leave to prove for 15 minutes and bake in a very hot oven (470 deg. gas 9) for about 15 minutes or until nicely brown. If liked, brush with melted butter or with beaten egg mixed with melted butter and a little milk as soon as you take them from the oven. Makes twelve.

These 'crestnuts' as D. calls them are delicious. A teaspoonful of sugar can be sprinkled over the crumbled yeast if desired. I always add it when my yeast goes a little dry through being kept for a few days (see page 102). Yeast is best stored in an earthenware cup and covered with greaseproof. I have also stored it successfully in my refrigerator. *This makes 12 croissants, each contains 15 gm. of carbohydrate.*

D.'S HOT CROSS BUNS

1 lb. plain flour sifted with a teaspoonful salt and a heaped teaspoonful mixed spice, 2 oz. pure lard or butter, 2 oz. each currants, mixed peel and sultanas, 1 oz. yeast, a level teaspoonful sugar, a good ½ pint tepid milk and water, a few pastry scraps rolled thin.

Rub the lard into the flour. Add the fruit, mix well and make a well in the centre. Crumble the yeast into the well, sprinkle the sugar over and pour in nearly all of the tepid liquid. Mix all to a moist dough adding the rest of the liquid if desired. Cover with a cloth and put to rise in a warm draught-free spot until double its bulk—about an hour. Turn on to a floured board, knead lightly and shape into buns. Brush with a little milk and put a cross of thinly rolled pastry on each bun. Leave to rise in a warm place 10–15 minutes and bake at 450 deg. for 10–15 minutes. Makes twelve or more buns. *Each of the 12 buns contains 30 gm. of carbohydrate.*

Weights and Measures

The American, and also the metric, equivalents of the British weights and measures used in these recipes are given below.

LIQUID MEASURES

The fluid ounce (fl. oz.) is the same in both Britain and America.

The British (or Imperial) pint = 20 fl. oz.
The American pint   = 16 fl. oz.

Measuring cups (liquid measure)

British breakfast cup   = 10 fl. oz. (½ Imperial pint)
British teacup   = 6⅔ fl. oz. (⅓ Imperial pint)
American standard cup = 8 fl. oz. (½ American pint)

Standard measuring spoons (liquid measure)

The American standard tablespoon and standard teaspoon are slightly smaller than their British equivalents.

8 British standard tablespoons   = 5 fl. oz.
10 American standard tablespoons = 5 fl. oz.
In each country, 3 teaspoons   = 1 tablespoon

1 British dessertspoon is approximately $\frac{1}{2}$ to $\frac{2}{3}$ of a tablespoon

APPROXIMATE METRIC EQUIVALENTS

Liquid measures

1 fl. oz.	= 28 millilitres (ml.)
1 British (Imperial) pint	= 570 ml.
1 American pint	= 450 ml.
1 litre	= $1\frac{3}{4}$ Imperial pints
	= $2\frac{1}{3}$ American pints

Weights

1 ounce (oz.)	= 28 grams (g.)
1 pound (lb.) (16 oz.)	= 454 g.
1 kilogram (kg.) (1000 g.)	= 2 lb. 3 oz.

Table of measurements for certain dry ingredients using American standard cup and tablespoon. Weight in ounces contained in:

Ingredient	1 cup	1 level tablespoon
Sifted flour	4	$\frac{1}{4}$
Caster sugar	7	$\frac{1}{2}$
Confectioners' or icing sugar	$4\frac{1}{2}$	$\frac{1}{4}$
Syrup, treacle, molasses	12	$\frac{3}{4}$
Rice (whole grain)	$7\frac{1}{2}$	$\frac{1}{2}$
Currants	$5\frac{1}{2}$	—
Fresh breadcrumbs	$2\frac{1}{2}$	—
Cornstarch or cornflour	—	$\frac{1}{3}$

Index

Index

Index